CATERING CZAR

The Life and Times of Jay Mastroianni,
Founder of *Jay's Catering*

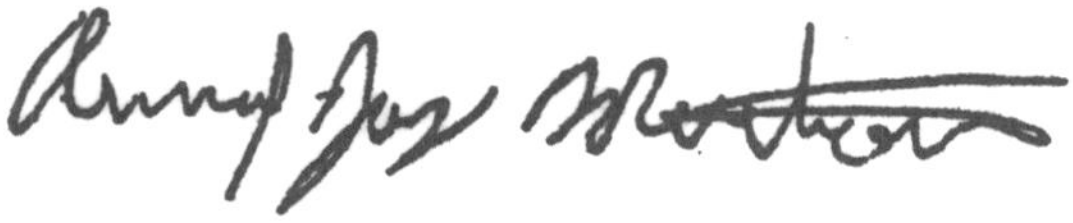

by
Armand Jay Mastroianni

with Roz Silva

International Standard Book Number: 13:978-0-615-14516-7

Library of Congress Cataloging-in-Publication Data is available.

First Printing, 2007

Jay-of-All-Trades Press
10581 Garden Grove Boulevard
Garden Grove, CA 92843
www.jayscatering.com

Printed in the United States

Book Design by m2design group

Dedication

Six months ago, I was a tired, old man who woke up between 10 and 10:30 a.m. and had my caregiver, Edith, drive me to *Jay's Catering*. If someone had already opened the mail, then I did not have anything to do. I would have lunch, clown around with the girls in the front office, and make my rounds visiting other employees. I went home at 2 p.m., took a nap, had dinner and went to bed by 7:30 p.m. It was a boring existence after all the things I had been used to in my lifetime. The truth is, I was depressed. The most I could do was dream of taking a vacation with my wife, but due to her illness, that was not possible.

Then one day, my daughter came to me to say she had made arrangements with my niece, Roz Silva, to help me write my memoirs. I thought she was nuts. I am not able to write things. I cannot spell. And besides, my niece lived 100 miles away. Linda decided that a tape recorder was the answer. I would tape my thoughts and Roz would transcribe them. I accepted my daughter's challenge because I never turn down a challenge. The fact that she had confidence in me to do this was amazing. My daughter loves me and I love her; we are very close, but we have our problems.

After she asked me to do this, I went to bed every night and spent every waking moment thinking about my life and the things that had happened to me—things that I had not thought about in years, and had even forgotten about—but it all came back. I remembered grade school, when I was 15 or 20 years old, the war, all the things we did at *Jay's*, and the progress we had made over the years. I believe it was God's will for me to write this book-- to leave a legacy to my family. I wanted my grandchildren to know their grandfather and their great grandfather, and to understand what we went through to get where we are today. It is to my dear family that I dedicate this book.

Contents

Chapter 1	New Beginnings	1
Chapter 2	How Mercury Savings Saved Me	3
Chapter 3	Settling In	5
Chapter 4	Recession-Proof? Not Me!	7
Chapter 5	Rebuilding From Scratch	9
Chapter 6	My Father, Giovanni Mastroianni	13
Chapter 7	A Bankruptcy Changes Things	15
Chapter 8	The War Years	19
Chapter 9	Back In Long Island	23
Chapter 10	The Amazing Eleanor	25
Chapter 11	Go West, Young Man, Go West	29
Chapter 12	Road Trip	33
Chapter 13	Elliot To The Rescue	37
Chapter 14	At Last, A Real Home	41
Chapter 15	Here We Grow Again	43
Chapter 16	Money In My Pocket Costs Me	45
Chapter 17	Hole-N-One	49
Chapter 18	Passing On The Dream	53
Chapter 19	Father Doesn't Always Know Best	57

Chapter 20	Los Caballeros	59
Chapter 21	Out Of Commission	61
Chapter 22	Invest In Yourself	63
Chapter 23	Under New Management	65
Chapter 24	Formula For Selling	67
Chapter 25	It's a Good Thing I Am The Boss	69
Chapter 26	Creative Genius	73
Chapter 27	The Kitchen—A 24-Hour Operation	77
Chapter 28	From Boys To Men	81
Chapter 29	Best Of The Best Parties	83
Chapter 30	Disasters—Some Averted, Some Not	87
Chapter 31	Valuable Lessons Learned	91
Chapter 32	I Love a Vacation	93
Chapter 33	Vacationing In New York On 9/11	95
Chapter 34	From 10 To 80 In 50 Years	97
Chapter 35	Who In The Family Will Succeed?	99
Chapter 36	Family Matters	101
Chapter 37	Near Death	103
Chapter 38	A Story Unfolds	105
Epilogue		107

Acknowledgments

I would like to thank my wife Eleanor for her support and guidance, my daughter Linda for her help and advice, and my sons John and Michael for fleshing out the story of Hole-n-One. Thanks to many others in the office, including Rose Imbriano, Barbara Breiter, Shellie Brison, and Betty Flati, for their unfailing contributions of administrative support and helpful input of every kind.

Of course, I am grateful to my niece Roz for the countless hours of transcribing tapes and making a guy like me sound so good on paper.

Heartfelt thanks also go to people who have helped me along the way on this journey toward reaching my goals. First and foremost, I have to thank Dr. Elliot Zaleznik, my benefactor; Ron Shankmen, who gave me my start with Mercury Savings & Loan, and Jack Klein, for introducing me to Dr. Z. I cannot forget Helen Conti, who helped me get started and proved to be the most important employee in the early days of Jay's Catering. I must thank the late Jerry Kobrin, former columnist of the Orange County Register, who dubbed me the "czar of catering," gave me much-appreciated press coverage, and introduced me to some very influential people.

Many thanks to Frank DeSantis for his friendship and the business he sent our way over the years; to Nick Palchikoff, a former administrator of Palm Harbor Hospital, who gave me my first wholesale milk account in 1958, and to Huntington Beach Superintendent of Schools Jack Roper for extending us the contract to run the Westminster and Huntington Beach High School cafeterias for several years. I cannot forget Dr. Sheldon Singer, a pillar in the community, who served as an unpaid salesman all these years, promoting my business and blessing me with his friendship. And finally, I want to thank our loyal customers who made our business the success it is today.

—Jay Mastroianni

Introduction

Soda jerk, shoe repairman, mill worker, service station attendant, milkman, 7-Up driver, independent distributor, truck caterer—these are the jobs I held on the way to becoming a self-made millionaire and catering "czar" of Orange County, Calif. I have experienced the joy of helping people plan memorable events—from weddings to bar mitzvahs, birthday to retirement parties, grand openings to company picnics, and every other type of social gathering. A dedicated family and a staff of hundreds work together to provide the preparation and planning, food and beverages, decorations and desserts for these special occasions in a person's life.

I could never have imagined that my multifaceted career would end here at Jay's Catering, my home away from home, the place I love to be. It is here that I find happiness and contentment, joy and excitement, challenges and creativity. I have also found friendship, loyalty, and people with big hearts. Through our doors have walked some incredible people—customers and friends alike. They continue to encourage us by their trust and stimulate us to do jobs in a bigger, better way. I am delighted I have been able to share my passion for serving others with my family, and am even more thrilled that I, along with my wife, have been able to pass this legacy on to my children and grandchildren. I hope that anyone who reads the story of my rise from ninth-grade dropout to successful businessman or "czar of catering," as I have been dubbed, will be inspired to persevere under the worst of circumstances and continue to follow their dreams, no matter what the obstacles. I did, and the results were well worth the struggle.

> *But if a man live many years and rejoice in them all: yet let him remember the days of darkness, for they shall be many.*
>
> —Ecc. 11:8

I

New Beginnings

I HAVE BEEN TO THE BRINK of both bankruptcy and death, but an impending bankruptcy dealt the bigger blow. I suppose that is because my most recent near-death experience left me on life support in a semi-conscious state for several weeks, oblivious to my condition. My dear wife and family suffered more. A subsequent re-habilitation was difficult since I had to learn to walk all over again, but in those five months, I also discovered how devoted my family was and how truly dedicated my friends were. The threatened bankruptcy was not so kind. It brought pain, shame, disillusionment and despair. However, as is often the case, when you are down and out, you learn that God never closes a door that He does not open a window. Through that window came a breath of fresh air in the form of the family business, Jay's Catering, that we enjoy today.

In 1958, my wife Eleanor and I packed our two children, Linda and John, in our 1953 Oldsmobile 88 and headed to Garden Grove, Calif., from a small Pennsylvania steel town. Within a week, I landed a job at Excelsior Creamery, delivering milk door-to-door in the bedroom communities south of Los Angeles. For the first time in my life, I made $100 a week! Eleanor, a registered nurse, went to work in the hospital emergency room of Palm Harbor Hospital and eventually became the Assistant Director of Nursing. Her job at the hospital proved to be a viable connection for my milk delivery business when the administrator, Nick Palchikoff, asked me if I wanted his hospital's milk business. I was delighted because I could make as much money from that one account as I could working all week for the dairy.

Due to his offer, I started my own business—delivering milk out of the trunk of my car until I could afford a truck. My business grew quickly as I continued to solicit other businesses and Nick referred me to four more hospitals in the area, which I also secured as customers. In 1967, I decided to rent an abandoned car wash in Midway City and convince my distributor, *Rockview Dairy,* to deliver milk to my depot, sparing me the 25-mile drive to retrieve it. Catering trucks stopped by to purchase dairy products from me, and it seemed like a good idea to open a supply house for the drivers. We began to buy our own catering trucks, and in no time, my company, Jay's Catering, owned a fleet of 37 trucks.

Customers at our depot inquired as to whether we would cater company and private Christmas parties. I enlisted the help of my wife, who happened to be a great cook, and we were off. She prepared Italian dishes, as well as sandwiches, salads and her signature carrot cake. By 1970, it became apparent that I needed Eleanor in the business full-time, so at my request and much to her dismay, she traded in her nursing cap for a chef's hat. Two years later, we built a facility in Huntington Beach, and won contracts to provide food service to three large school districts. After a vigilant campaign, I had also convinced *Mercury Savings & Loan* to allow me to cater their fledgling lunch program. These four large accounts, as well as 37 catering trucks on the road, helped propel me to the top and left me feeling very satisfied.

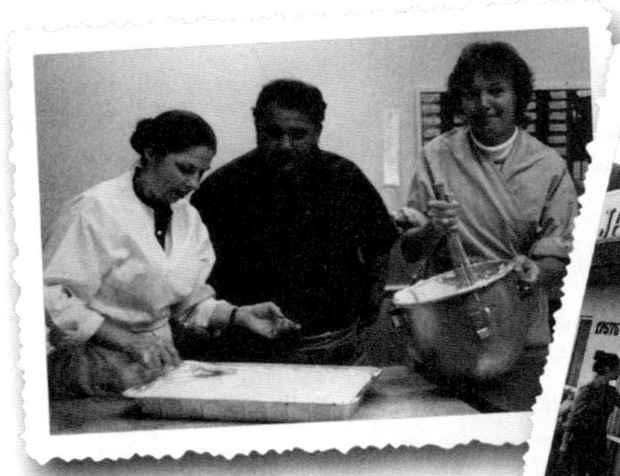

Kitchen workers show Jay carrot cake they prepared

Jay's original building in Huntington Beach

> *A desire accomplished*
> *is sweet to the soul.*
>
> —Prov. 13:19

2

How Mercury Savings Saved Me

Getting the Mercury account in 1972 was an especially satisfying achievement. I started "courting" Ron Shankmen, Vice President of *Mercury Savings and Loan* and President of the Huntington Beach School Board, by greeting him at the school board meetings. One night, he invited me to breakfast the next day. It took about a year of fraternizing, but he finally asked if I would like to take a shot at catering lunches at his bank. I was ecstatic. Landing this account would be as big as it was important to me. *Mercury Savings* invited local non-profit organizations to enjoy a free lunch in the bank's meeting room on the condition that the groups listen to a short presentation on the benefits of banking with *Mercury*. Previously, another caterer had prepared lunches in the traditional way, that is, having guests make their own sandwiches from the bread and lunch meat set on platters in front of them. That proved to be a very slow process given the short time allotted to feed a large group of people.

My wife and I had a better idea, but decided not to tell Ron what we were planning. On our first day as *Mercury's* caterer, we introduced our freshly, already-assembled turkey, ham and roast beef sandwiches, along with three salads, (potato, Cole slaw and *ambrosia*), a relish tray, and carrot cake for dessert. We took a gamble that our idea would work, and it did. This faster, more efficient way of serving people went over well—with *Mercury* and the lunch crowd. In addition, a wonderful thing happened to us when *Mercury* allowed us to put our business cards on the table. We received free advertising and subsequent business from those who attended daily lunches, experiencing our "cold buffet" at *Mercury's* seven or eight branches. *Mercury* reveled in its immensely popular lunch program and *Jay's Catering* found a built-in referral system for business. From then on, our phone never stopped ringing.

> *A time to gain*
> *and a time to lose.*
>
> —Ecc. 3:6

3

Settling In

At the same time I was working on establishing my business, I decided to join service organizations and become as involved in the community as I could—lessons I learned earlier from my brother-in-law, Frank Barco. The husband of my wife's sister Ann, he owned a coal and builder's supply business and had the respect of the whole community. He often ran for municipal offices in Pennsylvania and won, no matter what the position. In addition to his outgoing personality, Frank had a successful business, a wife and four children, a nice home, friends and money. In my eyes, he was probably the man I most wanted to be like, so I followed him around for a few years learning as much as I could.

After settling in Huntington Beach, Calif., I became vice president of the Parent Teachers Association at Westmont School, which my children attended. Fund-raising was one of my duties. We decided that Eleanor could use her culinary skills to cook spaghetti and meatballs for fund-raising dinners. The dinners were so successful that we raised more money for the PTA that year than had ever been collected before. The school appreciated the extra money, and the parents raved about Eleanor's cooking. They began to call our home asking us to cater parties and weddings. We never expected such a response to Eleanor's cooking, and it came as quite a surprise to us, but we took the challenge and started party catering on a small scale.

My community involvement took on other forms. First, I initiated the hiring of a crossing guard on Heil Street for the children at Westmont School, who were dodging cars on a very busy street by themselves. Next, I founded Pack 285 at the school and became its Cub Scout Master. As I delivered milk to homes in Huntington Beach, I began to get acquainted with the customers on my route and soon became well known in the community. I started attending city council meetings so I could learn the "Who's Who" in town and get myself known in those circles as well. In 1964, I ran for city council in Huntington Beach. There were 27 candidates and I finished tenth. It was a good thing I did not win because I did not know how to read very well and would have been the laughing stock of the town. Shortly thereafter, the mayor of Huntington Beach appointed me a commissioner of Parks and Recreation, and I served for about eight years. My name appeared in the newspaper on a regular basis as I chaired the "Save Huntington Beach" committee to oppose a city initiative.

I was popular enough in Huntington Beach that the national organization of the Sons of Italy asked if I would assist them in starting a local chapter. I agreed and worked hard to get members for the newly established Mare Vista Lodge, which, in English, means ocean view. Once organized, I was named the Venerable Jay Mastroianni—an impressive title for a guy who could not read. One night, I dreamt about a clambake, so I got busy putting together a real one. I ordered clams from the state of Washington, studied the proper way to steam them at the beach, and made arrangements with the Huntington Beach Superintendent of Beaches to allow us to serve beer and wine that night. My marketing skills led me to send flyers to every lodge in southern California, resulting in nearly 1,000 Sons of Italy members and their guests showing up for the clambake. It was one of the most notable events of the year! Later on though, without notifying the lodge's board of directors, and unaware that I had to follow protocol, I rented a storefront in Huntington Beach to serve as our headquarters for $100 per month. At the next meeting, the board reprimanded me for my actions. The club disbanded shortly thereafter.

The rest of our re-invented life was going as planned. My wife and I had a new life in a new place, with a profitable business, plenty of friends, and strong connections to the community, but things were about to change.

> *Better is a little with righteousness than great revenues without right.*
>
> —Prov. 16:8

4

Recession-Proof? Not Me!

The economy took a nosedive in 1973, and so did our lives. Before the recession that year, we had seven routes, averaging about $200 a day, servicing the *Mission Viejo Company*, builders of a new housing development in south Orange County. That may not seem like a lot of money, but in those days, coffee sold for 10 cents and a burrito was only a quarter. Within six months, when construction of new housing came to an abrupt halt, we dropped to one route. Of the 37 trucks, 15 were sitting idle, not generating any money, with payments due on them every month. In addition, the price of sugar rose from 10 to 75 cents a pound. I had a contract with three school districts to supply 4,000 pastry items per day. Each cost 11 cents and I sold them for 14 cents. In a very short time, my cost jumped to 27 cents each, but I could not increase the price to the schools for another seven months!

By the time the contract was up, I was heavily in debt to the dairy. Earlier, when I had needed financial help to purchase the trucks, I took on a partner and backer whose son had inherited the partnership after his father's death. I looked to my new partner to help me with additional funding. He chose not to put up the money, thus forcing me to surrender my business in late 1974. I lost everything, except one booking for the Huntington Beach Library Open House and my much-loved *Mercury Savings* account.

Submitting to my financial backer's decision to sell off the truck route catering business was devastating to me. I had worked so hard to build it. Besides, I had enjoyed a good reputation in the community and belonged to organizations like the Chamber of Commerce and the Exchange Club. I hung my head whenever I went anywhere because I was so embarrassed. I did not want to have to explain the situation with my financial backer since no one knew I had been in business with a silent partner. In fact, I left Huntington Beach and never looked back. The people I knew in the city never heard from me again. Every time I recognized someone from Huntington Beach, I turned around and walked the other way.

Facing my family was also painful. Until then, I had enjoyed my reputation as the "hotshot" brother living the good life in California. Considering the customary sibling rivalry that exists in families, I found it extremely difficult to tell them about my business failure. Yet, I knew I had to. I also knew that I would start over again. How else was I going to make a living?

One of Jay's Catering's 37 trucks

> *She rises while it is yet night.*
>
> —Prov. 31:15

5

Rebuilding From Scratch

The year was 1975. I was almost broke, and my future looked bleak. To make matters worse, I had broken my right arm when I fell off a ladder while cleaning leaves from the gutter. With pain and suffering on several levels, I turned my attention to *Mercury Savings*, the account I had worked so long and hard to acquire.

After losing the truck catering division, I planned to do everything I could to keep the lucrative part of my catering business. With the approval of *Mercury Savings* President, Leonard Shane, I would continue to service their account on my own, having dissolved my partnership and shedding the truck catering division. By laying off twenty people and getting rid of the expense of the underperforming truck routes, I cut my overhead tremendously. Of course, I had no working capital either.

To pull out of this serious financial setback, I borrowed $3,000 from my life insurance policy and $2,500 from a finance company. I enlisted the help of my family—my wife, daughter Linda, and youngest son Michael. (John was serving in the U.S. Army in Germany). I do not know how they managed, but Eleanor and Linda worked out of our house for nearly five months preparing food for the Mercury lunches. Eleanor awoke at 3 a.m.—just as my daughter arrived at our house. After they baked rolls and carrot cake, roasted the beef, ham and turkey, and mixed the salads, they packed everything in boxes. Hoping no one would find out that our house was our base of operation and the trunk of my car, our delivery truck, my son Mike and I dropped off the lunches to the banks five days a week. Amazingly, this one account, which became our "bread and butter" and sole source of income, brought in more profit than all 37 trucks!

As I got back on my feet, I bought a used truck for $400 and rented a 1,000 square foot building in Westminster. John was back from Germany and my family continued to work hard. Just when things were looking up, disaster struck again. This time it was a serious illness, which followed on the heels of three surgeries to restore my broken arm.

I had just returned from the gym with Dr. Elliot Zaleznik, an obstetrician I had met recently through *Mercury Savings'* vice presidents, Ron Shankmen and Jack Klein. They had introduced us in the early 1970s, and being a doctor, he quickly noticed the pain my still-unhealed arm was causing me and suggested we go to the local gym to soak in the Jacuzzi. From then on, Ron, Jack, Elliot, and I met at the gym two or three times a week to share a Jacuzzi. We joked about being three Jews and an Italian, and enjoyed getting to know one another. It was after one of those sessions at the gym that I fell ill. Noting a high fever, Elliot rushed me to the hospital and arranged for another doctor to treat me. The diagnosis was diverticulitis. I remained in intensive care for 42 days after the initial surgery and two others, which all occurred in a ten-day period. I was gravely ill and not expected to survive. At 45 years old, this would not be my last brush with death.

An interesting thing happened while I was in the hospital. As I was reading the newspaper, I learned that a man named Chuck Knox was the coach of the Los Angeles Rams football team. It occurred to me that I had a neighbor and friend by that name while living in Sewickley, Pa., years ago. I did not know if it was the same person since I had not seen or talked to him in over thirty years. My sister Rose knew Chuck better than I did because she ran the grocery store downstairs from the apartment building in which we all lived. When Rose realized it was our childhood friend, she rounded up all the people we knew in the Orange County/Los Angeles area and threw a party for him in her backyard. I was in the hospital awaiting a serious procedure and begged the doctor to let me out for one day so I could attend the party. He, of course, said "No," and I missed the big affair. Sometime later, when I was out of the hospital and feeling better, I was honored when Chuck asked if Jay's Catering wanted to provide food for the Anaheim Rams during training camp and practice sessions. We enjoyed catering for the players for a few years while Chuck was head coach. Just knowing Chuck Knox, an NFL Coach of the Year, and being able to say he was from my hometown meant a lot to me.

While all this was happening, my daughter Linda was pregnant with our first grandson, Michael. I prayed to God that he would let me live to see the baby born, and He did. My illness lasted over a year, and I lost almost 50 pounds while regaining most, but not all, the use of my right arm. My family stuck by me, as did Elliot, who visited with me several times a day at the hospital. One night after I had been sick for so long, I thought I heard a strange sound coming from within me. I was sure that my life was slipping away. I asked the nurse to call my wife so I could say good-bye to her. Eleanor rushed to the hospital and stayed with me throughout the night. Miraculously, I did not die, but lived to see another day. Although 30 years have passed, I can still remember the stress and difficulties associated with the early days of *Jay's Catering*, our family business. I also will never forget that it was my father, who instilled the idea of a family business in me as a child.

Jay and Dr. Elliot Zaleznik

Jay's father at 80

Giovanni (John) Mastroianni

Maria and Giovanni on their wedding day, December 25, 1918

A just man walks in his integrity, his children are blessed after him.

—Prov. 20:17

6

My Father, Giovanni (John) Mastroianni

My father, Giovanni (John) Mastroianni, was born in 1891 in Gizzeria, Italy, and lost his own father by the age of six. At 16, he went to Naples and boarded a ship bound for the United States—like the nearly 28 million immigrants who had flocked here from Italy at the turn of the Twentieth Century. When he arrived in New York City in 1907, he met an employment agent, who offered him work in a West Virginia coal mine for 10 cents an hour, on the condition he stay on the job for a minimum of two years. As soon as his two years were finished, my father headed for Long Island, New York, where friends from Italy had settled. My uneducated, impoverished father went to work as a gardener on huge Long Island estates, owned by wealthy men, like the Rockefellers, Whitneys, and Morgans.

After living in America for seven years, my father went back to Italy because of the war in Europe. He joined the Italian army and spent five years on the Austrian front. When he was discharged, he received a $2 mustering-out pay and went home to see his mother, only to learn that she had passed away. Shortly after that, he met and married my mother, Maria Perino, on Christmas Day, 1918. He returned to America, leaving his bride behind. It took another two years of gardening on the Long Island estates before he made enough money to send for her.

My parents had four children in five years, and I was the youngest. Born on September 15, 1929, I was named Ormando, after a WWI Italian general, Ormando Drazzo, but my family affectionately called me "Sonny." When I was three, my father became superintendent of Percy R. Pine's 35-bedroom mansion on 75 acres in Roslyn, Long Island, New York. Mr. Pine, one of Princeton University's biggest benefactors, provided us with a house on the premises, a station wagon, and an income of $190 a month. Being a natural-born leader, my father gained the respect of his employer and co-workers alike. As a superintendent, he was in a position to hire many of his friends to work the estate, which employed 40 gardeners and landscapers as well as chauffeurs and butlers. He also used his influence to get the local school board to start a night school where Italian immigrants, himself included, could learn English.

I wish I had more pleasant memories of my school days in Long Island, but I do not because of what happened in kindergarten. The earliest memory I have is the day my mother walked me to school. On the second day, my kindergarten teacher accused me of stealing cookies from another student. She placed a dunce cap on my head and made me sit in the corner behind the piano for a whole week. Can you believe that she did not allow me to participate in any activities the entire first week of school? I developed a very rebellious attitude in school for many years to come after being treated like a common criminal at the age of five.

My mother said good-bye to her mother when she was only 16 and never recovered from the heartache of leaving her and her homeland. She spent 20 years of her life in and out of hospitals—the last 13 in a nursing home. However, in her younger years, she did enjoy canning fruits and vegetables from the private gardens that Mr. Pine "let out" to my father and his friends. My mother was a great cook and taught my wife Eleanor how to make her favorite Italian dishes. Some of these same recipes are the ones that Eleanor perfected, with a little coaching from me, and has prepared for our customers since the beginning of our catering business.

It is likely that the seeds for the future *Jay's Catering* were planted in my mother Maria's kitchen in those days, but it was my father's example that spurred me on to success. This hard-working, family man urged me to some day build a business that would involve my family and help move us forward. He used to say, "As long as every generation improves, and your children have more than you did, then we are making progress."

As I was writing this chapter, it occurred to me that it has been exactly 100 years since my father left Italy to come to this beautiful country seeking a better life for his family. It gives me chills when I look back at where our family was then and realize how far we have come. I hope I made my father proud. I will always be grateful for what he did for me and how he provided, protected and supported my siblings and me.

A wise son makes a glad father.

—Prov. 15:20

7

A Bankruptcy Changes Things

In the summer of 1941, my father lost his job when his millionaire employer, Mr. Pine, filed bankruptcy. He reportedly incurred millions of dollars in losses on one day in the stock market. Out of work, my father decided to visit his brother-in-law in Sewickley, Pa., near Pittsburgh. In addition to Long Island, people from his hometown province of Calabria, Italy, had settled there. We had friends and connections in both places. Because the opportunities for employment were better in Sewickley, my father decided we would permanently stay there, much to my shock. At eleven, this had another devastating affect on me because I never had a chance to say good-bye to my friends and relatives in Long Island. Only my dad and my brother returned there to pack up our belongings and bring them back to Pennsylvania.

One thing he failed to bring back from Long Island was my final report card from my grade school. When my father enrolled me in the new elementary school, he had to place me in the 6th grade for a second year since there was no evidence I had truly graduated! I not only had to repeat 6th grade, but also had to deal with the discrimination I found in Sewickley, a small town seventeen miles northwest of Pittsburgh. At my new school, I discovered that each grade level had two classes, A and B. White Anglo-Saxon Protestant children filled Class A, while blacks, Italian, Polish, and other immigrants made up the B Class. This arrangement so irritated me that I could not concentrate and spent the year rebelling. My state of mind, coupled with being a marginal student to begin with, led to my failure of 6th grade, this time for certain. I entered Catholic school in the fall—only to retake 6th grade once again. Upon graduation from 8th grade at St. James', I went to Sewickley High School, which to my knowledge did not practice discrimination. In fact, while I was there, the school district hired Louie Visio, the first son of an Italian immigrant to teach at Sewickley High. In 9th grade, I made the football team. I stayed in school for the first three months during football season, but something happened after the season to change that. A teacher called on me to read in front of the class, and since I could not comfortably do so, I closed my book, walked out of the classroom and out of school for good.

After that, my father grabbed me by the hand and took me to his friend, who owned the local shoe repair shop. He said to Mr. Macaluso, "This is my son; he's no good in school, so I want you to please teach him a trade." He wanted me to become a shoemaker, which I did. I worked for Mr. Macaluso for two years, shining shoes and replacing heels. Although I was good at what I did, I hated it, particularly when I got shoe polish on my hands and under my nails. Dirty hands were an embarrassment when it came to meeting girls!

By the end of two years, I looked for another job that paid more than $2 a week. Unlike Mr. Macaluso, who kept me in my place so as not to pay me more, Jack Prince offered me $5 a week and mentored me as well. At *Prince Shoe Repair*, I learned to shine shoes like Mr. Hickenbottom, the best shoeshine man around at that time. This man had a talent like no other. He was adept at shining black or brown and white saddle shoes, popular in the day, which were difficult to shine because of the contrasting colors on the straps of leather across the instep. I decided to learn from him so I could bring in the kind of tips he did. Shortly, the promise of more money necessitated a move to another shop in Coraopolis, Pa., where I worked for Louie Gilberti, winner of a national shoe repairman contest that year. Although I entered, I did not win. Mr. Gilberti had a passion for great shoe repair work, but to me, it was just a job.

Mastroianni siblings and cousins in New York

Jay at age 9

Long Island School

A family gathering at an aunt's house in Brooklyn, New York

> *A foolish son is a grief to his father.*
>
> —Prov. 17:25

8

The War Years

On Sunday, December 7, 1941, as I was walking home past Sewickley High, I heard shouting. People were yelling that the Japanese had bombed Pearl Harbor. Scared, I ran home as fast as I could to tell my parents. These family-minded, uneducated people soon realized that their 17-year-old son, my brother Amo, would be going to war. He shipped out to England as part of the 2nd Infantry, serving as a lineman, in charge of communication from the front of the line to the back. My brother fought long and hard for this country and received a Purple Heart for his efforts at Normandy on D-day. Of the 220 members of his company, he was one of only 28 men who survived that infamous battle without injury. He continued his duty in Austria, Czechoslovakia, France, and Denmark and was decorated by the Russians for "Outstanding Bravery." He received three Bronze Stars for his efforts at Normandy, the Battle of the Bulge and in Czechoslovakia.

After the victory in Europe, Amo came home on R&R. He was skinny as a rail and looked pale and drawn. While my brother was on leave, I turned seventeen and decided to follow his example and join the army myself. It was near the end of World War II, but it was not over yet. In those days, induction into the armed services was quick and easy. When you showed up at the recruiting office and if you passed your physical, you were inducted the same day. On the day I planned to leave, I dressed and stopped at the top of the staircase of our two-story home to say good-bye to my brother. I reached to hug and a kiss him good-bye when

Grace, Rose, Amo and Jay

he suddenly punched me and threw me down the stairs. With a sprained arm and a bruised face, I asked him why he wanted to hurt me. He replied, "I fought enough in the army for both of us, and you're not leaving here. If you do, I will kill you!" I believed him.

At that point, I did not know where to turn. With no job, and the army not an option, I found work in a gas station for $20 a week in Belview, twelve miles from Sewickley. There was no safe at the station, so the person who closed up had to take the money home and bring it back the next morning. Sewickley was a typical small town, a mere one square mile in area —with nearly 1,000 wealthy people living in Sewickley Heights, and about 4,000 Italians, Caucasian, Blacks and Polish living in the rest of the town. The local barbershop sported a pool table and poker table in the back room. At 15 or 16, I became a regular there, and no one seemed to mind since all the older boys were off fighting a war. I gambled and shot pool. When I was not in the pool hall or gambling, I was bowling or dancing, which is what I liked most. Every weekend, bands played in the three dance halls in the areas, and I loved going there.

I got into a lot of mischief in those days and spent some wild years. Once, I took my father's car when he left the keys in it. I was only 16 and my father would not let me get a license because my brother had three accidents the first year after he got his! I took the car and drove it for 2 or 3 miles on the rails of the streetcar, which went to Pittsburgh. After that, my father sold the car and rode a bicycle to work!

Another time, when I got off the bus in front of the barbershop where I hung out, I had $300 in gas station receipts on me. There was a blackjack game going on and I made a quick decision to get in on it. Unfortunately, I lost the $300 and did not know how I was going to pay it back until I remembered my father's friend, Tom Perry. Mr. Perry, an importer of oil and grapes, was quite a wealthy man and a friend of the whole family. He also was my only hope! He had a son of his own, and I knew that if the situation were reversed, my father would help Mr. Perry's son. At 3 a.m., I yelled to him from outside his apartment and asked if he would lend me $500. He told me to come upstairs, and upon hearing my story, gave me the money. I begged him not to tell my father for fear he would kill me, and I believed Mr. Perry would keep the secret. The next day, I replaced the money in the cash register and spent a hundred dollars on a train ticket to New York.

Eventually, I realized that it would take me years to pay back Mr. Perry since the most I was making was $20 a week. I summoned up the courage to tell my father what I had done. Since enough time had elapsed, my father got over his anger quickly, forgave me, and settled my debt with Mr. Perry!

He that labours,
labours for himself;
for his mouth
craves it of him.

—Prov. 16:26

9

Back In Long Island

I headed for my Aunt Frances' Long Island home, and she invited me to stay with her. I called my parents to tell them I was back in New York and planned to stay there. Soon, I got a job at a shoe repair shop in Glen Cove, Long Island, for $20 a week. I worked there for quite awhile, but it was too far to travel every day, so I found a job closer to home in Garden City—home of *Doubleday Books*, across from the world-renowned Garden City Hotel. The Caballa family employed me for 6 to 8 months while their son was serving in the U.S. Army.

They treated me like a son, but had to let me go when their own son came home. Oddly enough, with his financial help, I bought a shoe repair shop for $1,000 in Linbrook, New York. Since it was a Jewish community, I named my shop *Norman's* in keeping with the ethnicity of the neighborhood. No one ever questioned an Italian kid doing business in a Jewish neighborhood. Frankly, at 17 ½, I was not ready to run a shop, nor did I know how to deal with people. Within a year, I also began selling dress and work shoes. Being a novice in the business, I did not realize that if I bought 300 pair of shoes, I would never sell all of them. I ended up giving them away or putting them on sale.

About two years later, there was an opportunity to move to a new area, called Massapequa Park, the Levittown of Long Island. I did fairly well there but was still not mature enough to be in business for myself. I found it impossible to increase my cash flow, partly because I spent too much money on socializing and going out on the town.

One of the dumbest things I ever did happened while I was driving on the Long Island Expressway. I had recently purchased a 1930 4-door, 6-wheel, 12-cylinder Cadillac convertible for $60 and wanted to show it to my brother—in Pittsburgh. Impulsively, I headed west. The car made it all the way to Harrisburg, Pa., about a five-hour drive, before the motor burned up. Since I did not have the money for repairs, I had to leave the car at a repair shop. When the owner offered me $15 for the car, I took it, on the condition that he return the brand new suit jacket I had left in the car. He never did. I think that car would be worth a hundred thousand dollars today. I traveled the rest of the way by bus to Pittsburgh, where my brother met me. He kept introducing me as his brother with a $60 car and a $100 suit. I decided it was time to move back to the Pittsburgh area and bring my mother and father, who had followed me to Long Island earlier, with me.

By that time, I considered myself a bona fide shoe repairman, so I applied for a job at *Boggs & Buell,* a department store on the north side of Pittsburgh. They hired me as a relief man to cover vacations and other absences in locations all over the country. I traveled to cities like Detroit, Mich., and Mansfield and Steubenville, Ohio, just to name a few. The shop in Steubenville was located across the street from the *Rex Café*, the gambling casino where Dean Martin got his start. Not legally old enough to enter the casino, I never saw Martin perform, but I heard all about him. I enjoyed the traveling. Being single, I was not leaving behind a family and had the opportunity to see more of the country.

Jay's shoe repair shop "Norman's" in Linbrook, NY

"Whoso finds a wife finds a good thing, and obtains favor of the Lord."

—Prov. 18:22

10

The Amazing Eleanor

I MET MY WIFE, then Eleanor Rubino, at *Conway's Corner* in Rochester, Pa., in 1953 when I was 23. I bravely asked her for the last dance of the evening at nearby McDaniel Hall. She said, "Yes," and off we went. I fell in love with her that night and never let her out of my sight after that. Not too many days later, she introduced me to her mother. I could not believe it when her mother, Mrs. Rubino, said, "If you aren't going to marry my daughter, get the hell out of here!" Although I did not respond to her, I did stick around because I knew in my heart that someday I would make her daughter my wife. Soon, I began to meet Eleanor's brothers and sisters—all ten of them living in a two-bedroom house. They lived in crowded conditions, but got along very well; their love for one another filled the small, wood-frame house, located across the street from a noisy train station.

Eleanor began to apologize for being poor—as though that would discourage me. I was so proud of her for finishing nursing school, despite the obstacles she faced. She had the persistence and fortitude to follow her dreams, and I knew that she was the person with whom I wanted to spend the rest of my life.

Eleanor's parents, Sam and Jenny Rubino, were married in Italy on December 4, 1911. As was the custom, theirs was an arranged marriage, and after only two months, my father-in-law, at the encouragement of his relatives in America, ventured across the ocean. He joined his relatives in Raton, New Mexico, to work in the silver mines. Four years later, Jenny traveled the same road to New Mexico, where she settled down and started a family with Sam. In no time, the couple had three children. Sam heard from other relatives in Coraopolis, Pa., about the booming steel industry in nearby Pittsburgh. When work slowed in the silver mines, he decided to take advantage of work opportunities there and moved with his family to Coraopolis. After six years there and three more children, Sam and Jenny settled in Monaca, Pa., where they lived until their deaths.

Sam worked at *Colonial Steel* for 42 years as a furnace fireman, and in his later years, as a mill hand. During those four decades, no matter the condition of his health, he walked the two and a half miles to and from work in all kinds of weather – heat and humidity, rain (with no umbrella) or snow (with no boots). This gentle soul always worked for minimum wage, which made it very difficult to feed and clothe their children. In spite of the financial hardship, in the next six years, Jenny gave birth to five more children, including my wife, Eleanor. She was born in October 1931—in the midst of the Great Depression.

Eleanor's mother, Jenny, was a hardworking woman, who cooked, cleaned, washed clothes and supervised all eleven children every day of the week. Jenny, a proud woman, strove for perfection in all her children and encouraged them to get an education, which was a privilege in those days. The four-year absence of her oldest son, Tony, who was 18 when he joined the U.S. Army during World War II, hurt the family financially. Later, her 16-year-old daughter, Rosie, was stricken with Hodgkin's disease, and suffered for five long years before her death. Since there was no such thing as medical insurance, it took the family five more years to pay off the enormous medical debt. Every one of the children, including Eleanor, had to help somehow.

Jenny sent Eleanor to work at the tender age of ten. Eleanor traveled by bus or in a "jalopy", driven by a cousin, to neighboring towns four or five miles away to help clean house for her mother's relatives with small children. During summer vacation, Eleanor spent day and night doing chores and keeping house for others.

When Eleanor was 14 or 15 years old, she worked at *Conway Corner's*, the restaurant in Rochester, Pa., where I met her. Because she did not have enough money for bus fare both ways, she usually walked the mile and a half to work, and rode the bus home after midnight. Her employers, Elsie and George Milianos, took Eleanor under their wing. George even taught her how to drive—a privilege her family could not afford. Again, Eleanor handed over her paycheck to her mother.

After high school, Eleanor enrolled at Providence Hospital School of Nursing. She continued to work nights and weekends in order to pay for living essentials. However, her work began to have a negative effect upon her grades, so Eleanor planned to quit school. An instructor at the nursing school heard of her plight and offered to lend her the money to continue her nursing career. She accepted his offer and graduated from nursing school in 1952.

The following year, Eleanor and I were married on July 25, 1953. I borrowed $500 from my brother to pay for our wedding. After the 9 a.m. church service, we went to the Sons of Italy Hall in Monaca, Pa., where we served lunch to about 100 guests. I paid five women $5 a piece to cook the meal and buy the groceries. The meal, consisting of spaghetti, sausage, chicken, salad and a traditional wedding soup, cost about $100. Our reception was held that evening in Ambridge, Pa., at the Polish Hall. It was a hot, humid night and there was no air conditioning.

We did not have a dinner, but instead served 1,500 ham sandwiches made with hamburger rolls and mustard, wrapped in parchment and placed in wax paper bags. One server held a bushel basket full of the sandwiches while the other one handed out the sandwiches. In most cases, the sandwiches were thrown to the guests, much like they throw t-shirts at baseball games today. Beer and soda were readily available.

When I got married almost 54 years ago, I had never even heard of a caterer, let alone aspired to be one. You would have to agree that our service is better than it was in those days!

After the reception, we opened our gift envelopes so I could re-pay my brother—making us several hours late checking in to Pittsburgh's Roosevelt Hotel for our honeymoon night! It was a wonderful night even if we were delayed. From there, we drove to Atlantic City, New Jersey, in my $350, 1946 4-door Plymouth and down the coast to Cape May, where I sampled clams from the numerous clam bars along the way, before heading back to Long Island, to visit my Aunt Frances and Cousin Dominic. Eleanor and I decided to go home three days early because we felt we should spend money on things we needed for our apartment, instead of on a longer honeymoon.

Eleanor relaxing on our honeymoon

Our wedding picture

My 1946 Plymouth —our honeymoon get-away vehicle

A good name is rather to be chosen than great riches.

—Prov. 22:1

II

Go West, Young Man, Go West

For the first few years after our marriage, we lived next door to my brother in Rochester, Pa. Eleanor and I were able to buy a little house for $6,000, with the help of my father, who provided a down payment of $2,000. Then, I was a 23-year-old young man trying to make his way in the world and not the same person I am today.

Aside from Frank Barco, my brother Amo was my main role model, but that bothered Eleanor. She thought I should make my own life instead of depending on my brother so much. My brother and I both had dropped out of school in the ninth grade. He got a job working in a gas station and eventually became good friends with the owner of the station. After the war, Amo bought the gas station with money my father loaned him. I worked for my brother for about four years even though I knew I took no pleasure in being a mechanic or service station attendant. Once, I ran his tow truck over the side of a hill, smashing it; another time, I drove his brand new car through a stop sign and wrecked it. When working on one of his best customer's cars, I drained the oil and forgot to replace it. Of course, the motor burned up, and my brother had to pay for a new one. I began to get a complex, as I realized that I was not cut out for that line of work. I had not discovered my niche in life, and had to keep searching for a few more years. I think I found it in California, thanks to Eleanor.

She wanted us to start a life of our own. When the state of Pennsylvania exercised eminent domain in 1958, forcing us to sell our house, we faced the decision of where to move. After paying bills from the $8,000 profit on the sale, we still did not have enough for a down payment on a decent house in the area. Eleanor suggested we move instead to California! She had heard about the job opportunities from my sister, who was already living in southern California. I wanted to stay in Pennsylvania to be near my mother and brother, but Eleanor encouraged me to strike out on my own. That decision changed our lives forever and provided us with unbelievable opportunities.

We arranged to leave for California on December 8, 1958. My sister was kind enough to rent us a house directly behind her. I sent her the $90 a month rent and had our furniture sent by moving van. These days you cannot move your furniture across the street for the $445 it cost us to send our belongings cross-country!

The night before we left, our families gathered at my brother-in-law Ted's place for a huge send-off. Everyone came to say good-bye and it was exciting to know we were leaving the next day. Early in the morning, with our kids in tow, we got in the car and headed west toward Columbus, Ohio. I had planned to take Route 66 from there, but the eight inches of snow on the ground changed my mind. I looked at the map to find an alternative route and decided to go south through the Blue Ridge Mountains of Kentucky, which is probably the most beautiful route I have ever driven. The mountains were great to behold and the horizon, breathtaking. From there we went through Texarkana, Texas, and on to Dallas. We drove into New Mexico to visit Carlsbad Caverns. We stayed for a while, touring the caverns and enjoying a wonderful family time with our little ones, Linda and John. The two of them were well behaved the entire trip, considering they were in a car for 3,000 miles. Then we passed through El Paso on a two-lane road that ran alongside the mountains. The scenery was incredible and looked like the place where they film old-fashioned Western movies. Our route took us to Yuma, Ariz., an interesting place I have always wanted to visit but never have.

My memory of the rest of the trip was one of driving through a sand dune. There was sand everywhere. Emerging from the sand, we drove into Riverside, Calif., on another two-lane road, and not the freeway that runs through it today. It was a thrill to see this very old town with its historic, mission-style buildings. Our hearts raced as we realized that we were a mere 35 miles from Orange County. Getting more excited by the minute, we could not wait to see where we would be living. We counted down the miles, but nothing but orange trees and mountains were visible for the last twenty miles. Traveling Route 91, we finally ended up at the circle in the city of Orange. It was our first glimpse of a populated area. In the late 1950s, there were about 700,000 people in the entire county. Today, Orange County has a population of over 3 million, and we have been witness to the growth that has taken place over the last 50 years.

Our trip took about a week from coast to coast. We went directly to our house, with furniture in place, thanks to my sister. It was fantastic to drive across the country and move in the same day we arrived. On Christmas Day, we had dinner in my sister's backyard, under sunny skies and a temperature that reached 85 degrees. What a shock to our system that was, having spent our former Christmases in Pennsylvania, where it is usually 25 to 30 degrees and snowing!

John, Jay, Linda and Eleanor, December 1958

And he said, Let us take our journey, and let us go, and I will go before thee.

—Gen. 33:12

12

Road Trip

That extraordinary trip to California carries more pleasant memories than the roundtrip experience we had a year and a half later when we received a phone call notifying us that my father had had a stroke. We were still lonely and missed our families immensely, thus Eleanor and I decided to go back to Pennsylvania to see my dad. We had no money for airfare; driving cross-country was our only option. I do not remember how much money I had, but since an American Express card did not exist in those days, I had to have cash, or simply not go. Within 24 hours, we began our 3,000-mile road trip in my almost-new, 1959 Ford Galaxy—with no air conditioning.

It was August, and our son Michael was only eight months old. John was about five and Linda, six. We traveled as far as Needles, Calif., where it was 100 degrees at nightfall, before we had a flat tire. In fixing the flat, I learned that the tires were wearing on one side, and realized that if I had still had thousands of miles to go, then I had better replace all the tires. The price of the new tires cost me almost all the money I had. I knew I could rely on my brother to lend me money for the return trip, but it was the last thing I wanted to do—admit I did not have enough money to get back to California. I cannot recall if he wired me money or I waited until I arrived in Pennsylvania to ask him, but I know he did provide the necessary funds.

We continued on to Las Vegas, Nev., where the temperature was 120 degrees. Michael was so hot that my wife was frantic he would get sick. Somehow, we made it to Pennsylvania and enjoyed a nice visit with my father, whom I had missed terribly. Even though we suffered miserably on the road, it was all worth it because I saw my dad.

We were there a few days when my sister-in-law Dorothy decided to move to California to be with her husband, Jesse, who had made the trip to California earlier to "seek his fortune." Since she did not have money for airfare, she and her daughter, Marilyn, would drive back with us. Taking into account the weather conditions (the heat) on the southern route, I planned to drive through Colorado and Utah, over the Rocky Mountains, where the altitude reached 15,000 feet, and then through Nevada into California.

To carry my sister-in-law's luggage, I rented a container for the top of the car. When I kept running out of gas every few miles, I thought the container was causing the car to use more gas since it was providing drag. At that time, gasoline cost $0.20 a gallon and a $100 worth of gas would take you across the country. However, averaging 7 or 8 miles to a gallon through the Rockies, I realized I would spend a lot of money, even at that rate. It was also frightening going up and down the mountains as my car sputtered and coughed in the higher elevations. I stopped at a gas station and asked the attendant to check to see if the container was the problem. Upon inspection, he informed me that the gas tank was leaking, particularly when we went up the mountain. I had no choice but to have the tank fixed.

Now, I had $8 in my pocket. At the beginning of the trip, I had purchased a portable stove that we could use to barbecue hot dogs at a rest stop in case we did not have enough money to eat in restaurants. With seven hungry people to feed and next to no money, we bought hot dogs and found a picnic area. Unfortunately, the stove did not work, but it was so hot—114 degrees—that I was able to roast those hot dogs on a big rock, with the sun providing the energy.

When we pulled into Las Vegas, I could go no further without some rest. I was exhausted from the drive and the heat of the Mojave Desert, and so was everyone else. Dorothy had $15 left, and we used $8 to pay for one hotel room for all seven of us. By the time we got home, we were completely out of food and money. The trip was such a nightmare that it ranks right up there as one of the worst experiences of my life.

One of the more pleasant memories of that horrendous trip was how Dorothy, being the entertainer that she is, started singing with the kids. We all sang a song that used the same pattern, with different letters of the alphabet. It went something like this:

"B-A, BAY, B-E, BE

B-I, Bickey Bi

B-O, BO

Bickey Bi, Bo

B-U, Bu

Bickey, Bi, Bo, Bu"

Luckily, that song kept the kids occupied all the way across the Midwest, although it drove me crazy. We have never taken that trip by car again, although we have traveled to Pennsylvania many times since then. Besides, my journey to becoming a self-employed businessman was about to take up a lot of my time, which brings me back to 1975, where I left off to tell the story of my early years.

The 1959 Ford Galaxy which took us cross-country

> *A friend loveth at all times and a brother is born for adversity.*
>
> —Pro. 17:17

13

Elliot To The Rescue

If it was my father's encouragement to go into a family business, then it was my friend Elliot's trust in my vision that made the catering business we have today possible.

Our Mercury lunch account continued to grow and we began servicing a second bank, which offered the same kind of free lunch program. In 1975, I had an opportunity to rent a larger building on Brookhurst Street in Garden Grove, but since I was still recovering from the losses connected to my truck catering business, I did not have the money to make the move. It only made sense to ask my friends at *Mercury Savings* if their bank would lend me the money. Unfortunately, they informed me that due to my poor credit rating, the bank could not. Three months later, while we were once again sitting in the Jacuzzi, I mentioned my cash flow problem to Elliot. Without hesitation, he blurted out, "How much do you need? I've got the money; I can lend it to you." He then wrote me a check for $250,000 unsecured. It was incredulous that he would make such a generous loan, considering I could not borrow a nickel from the bank!

My relationship with Elliot blossomed into a true friendship. I invited him to my house to meet my wife. She cooked him a dinner of spaghetti and meatballs, but Elliot said, "I won't come anymore unless I get turkey sandwiches. They're my favorite." After that, whenever Elliot came to dinner, Eleanor cooked spaghetti, meatballs and served our turkey sandwiches. Elliot and I have remained good friends all these years, but he has since retired to Florida. Recently, I got a phone call from him and he said, "Jay, I need some turkey sandwiches. Do you know how I can get them?" I assured him I would send them via FedEx until he explained he was merely joking. He talked to Eleanor about her recent diagnosis of breast cancer and helped relieve some of her fears. That is the way Elliot is—a caring, concerned friend. When my grandson Michael was born, we called him at midnight to report my daughter Linda was in labor at the hospital. He went to the hospital, checked on her, and came to our house to wait. He proceeded to lie down on the couch and wait for a call from the hospital. We never got a bill from him for the delivery or for the office visits and health care he provided to Linda and my wife regularly from then on.

Some people questioned why Eliott would lend me a quarter of a million dollars unsecured. As I have already said, I could not understand it either, but he did. When we first met, and for reasons I still cannot explain, Elliot and I became fast friends. We found we had a lot in common. We were both sons of immigrants—the difference being that his parents were from Russia, and mine, from Italy. We had similar childhoods and enjoyed sharing stories about our heritage. Elliot spoke of being poor, but also remembered how hard his mother had worked to put him through school. This was a case of a Jewish mother wanting her son to be educated so he could make something of himself. Elliot did. He became a doctor and made more money that he ever dreamed possible. Having been poor, he did not flaunt his wealth. Elliot drove a Plymouth Valiant back and forth to work. One day, he had to make an important phone call before he got to the hospital. He stopped at a gas station, and asked if he could call the hospital, but the attendant would not let him use the phone, probably noticing the coat hanger in the place of his car's antenna! I was a big spender but did not have the cash to back up my spending. Elliot, on the other hand, was much thriftier but had all kinds of cash. After telling me the story about his old Plymouth, he came by to show me the new Cadillac he had purchased and reported that he was also the proud owner of a late-model sports car. He asked if I was happy, and I said, "Yes, you deserve it."

One time we went skiing together at Mammoth, but drove separate cars. We were caught in an avalanche on the way up the mountain and spent the night in our cars waiting to be rescued. I was driving a 1977, four-wheel drive Cadillac, and my wife, who smoked then, needed a cigarette, but her pack was in the trunk. I got out to get her cigarettes during a blizzard, and the wind blew the trunk up in the air so hard that it sprung. When we finally left the ski resort, Elliott followed me down the mountain and kept blowing his horn to stop me. "What do you need?" I asked. He said, "I left my $40 boots up on the mountain and need to borrow your car to go get them." I said, "Hell no, let's just get off this mountain and forget those boots." We did have a good time despite everything that happened that weekend.

I do not know why Elliot was so generous. I do know that I was definitely out of my league. He was a doctor, and I only had an eighth grade education, a fact that has embarrassed me all my life. That did not seem to bother Elliot though.

He believed in me and took a risk that paid off—for all of us. I will never forget what he did for my family and me. The fact that Elliot and I are still friends would indicate that I did pay back his loan, with interest, of course!

"Seest thou a man diligent in his business, he shall stand before kings: he shall not stand before mean men."

—Pro. 22:29

14

At Last, A Real Home

The building Elliot's loan made possible was a 3,000 square foot storefront at 12222 Brookhurst Street in Garden Grove, and part of an 11,000 square foot building, owned by *Marinello Beauty School.* I was sincere when I told the owner that someday I would buy the whole building, not just lease it. From the moment we moved in, *Jay's Catering* made money. The type of catering we did was not difficult. We had a limited menu and served a middle-class clientele. We provided large amounts of good-tasting food at reasonable prices, and it proved to be a recipe for success. We also had a full-time interior decorator, who doubled as a cake decorator, on staff. From the very start of our association, Helen Conti worked harder than anyone I know and became not only a valued employee, but also a trusted friend. Helen made sure that the decorations at every party were as special as our food. Her excellent taste and our delicious food proved to be a winning combination. With the help of her husband, who did the construction, she even designed the façade of our building.

In 1975, our first year in that building, we saw an increase from $240,000 to $500,000 in sales. By the third year, our sales topped $1 million. We continued to grow year after year and never did a bit of advertising. More business came through word-of-mouth referrals than any other way. I maintained my involvement in the community and discovered that those close ties were better than any paid advertising.

In addition to moving the business to Garden Grove, I decided to purchase a home there that would be suitable for entertaining. My objective was to design the perfect party house where I could demonstrate how a party should be done. I enlisted Helen as my decorator, and she transformed our new house into a model party home amenable to all types of entertaining. The traffic flow and size of my home allows us to serve a sit-down dinner for 50 or 60 people comfortably, a buffet for 75 people, or an elegant party for 100 to 120 people where hors d' oeuvres are passed. During the 30 plus years we have lived on Woodward Circle, we have hosted more than 100 events, including civic fund-raisers, Chamber of Commerce and Kiwanis dinners, and private parties. In 1988, we were proud to accept Garden Grove Home of the Year Award, bestowed on us by the city.

From the affairs we have hosted in our home, we have been able to "show and tell" our guests just what our catering business can do for them, and have obtained a large volume of business this way. In addition, by living in the same town where our business is located, we have maintained a positive presence in the community, sponsoring and supporting programs to assist children and the elderly, as well as donating food, time and money whenever possible. Over the years, the community has responded by recognizing us several times. Actually, the first award I received was "The Heritage Pioneer Award" from the American Italian Renaissance Foundation" in 1988 for outstanding contributions to our heritage. Then in 1996, Eleanor and I were the recipients of the Garden Grove Chamber of Commerce Community Achievement Award, and in 2002, we received an Orange County Ethics in America Award, bestowed by Chapman University's Leatherby Center for Entrepreneurship and Business Ethics. I was humbled when friends and colleagues at the Garden Grove Chamber of Commerce named me "Man of the Year" in 2004. Moving our business to Garden Grove in 1975 proved to be the beginning of a long and happy relationship with the people of this city, and once again, Eleanor and I have enjoyed the opportunity to be active members of it—which has always been one of my aspirations.

*12222 Brookhurst St.
Garden Grove*

> *But in a great house, there are not only vessels of gold and of silver, but also of wood and of earth...*
>
> —II Tim. 2:20

15

Here We Grow Again

Firmly established as the "sandwich caterer of Orange County," I dreamt about the day I would become the caterer that people called on for their every party need. I was envious of my competitors who serviced the elite and hoped to be able to do the same someday. I knew it would be difficult to change our image, but I was certainly going to try. However, when an opportunity arose to do an "upscale" party, we did not have the necessary tables, chairs or other items and had to rent them from companies that carried such things. Even though these companies granted me a 15% discount, I quickly discovered it was not profitable because of the labor involved in transporting, tracking and returning the items in working order. Considering our clientele, I did not want to have to charge an additional rental fee as other caterers were doing.

Instead, I figured that the smartest thing I could do was to buy my own equipment. If I bought an item for $100, then rented it for $20, it would pay for itself after only five rentals. Everything after that was "gravy." Owning our rentals has proved to be a very profitable part of our business. Because we have such a large inventory, we are able to provide our customers with almost anything they request. This has allowed us to remain competitive and acquire many outstanding jobs, especially over the last fifteen years, since Linda has improved and categorized our inventory.

We not only began to own rental equipment, but just as predicted, I was offered the chance to own the building we leased. The property owner, *Marinello Beauty*

School, offered to sell it to me in 1983 and agreed to a nine-month escrow. I put $40,000 down and paid the balance at the close of escrow. Eventually, a bank appraisal revealed that the building was worth $550,000 or two times more than the $275,000 I paid for it.

The following year, the city of Los Angeles hosted the 1984 Summer Olympics. I had recently hired a public relations agency, *Ginter & Associates*. The owner, DeDe Ginter, handled our bid to secure Olympics business, and amazingly, we won the bid on the food concession for nine of the VIP venues! That amounted to a half million dollars worth of business in July of 1984. In addition, the city of Carson was opening a new community center. My daughter Linda asked DeDe to work up a bid on that catering concession as well. While DeDe dug up demographics and other facts about Carson that could help secure the $1 million account, I was busy working on personal marketing and presentation. Our biggest competitor was a company from Long Beach that owned a hotel. In addition to meeting other criteria, we had to cater a party for several hundred people, as did our competitor. The differences between our two parties were huge, so we won easily. *Jay's Catering* clinched the account by using good quality food from our limited, inexpensive "mom and pop" menu. Everything we prepared was "handmade" in our kitchen, while our rival offered commercially prepared hotel food. That was over 20 years ago and fortunately, most hotels today have greatly improved the quality of their catering.

Although we outbid and outshone our competitor, the city of Carson decided to give them a piece of the pie. Much to our shock, the city hired the two men who worked for the hotel to run the community center! Since they were professionals and more knowledgeable about banquets, it was agreed that they would hire personnel, schedule events and generally oversee the banquet facility, while *Jay's* would be in charge of the food. No longer competitors, we have worked together for over twenty years. We must re-negotiate our contract each time it comes up for renewal, and although many have tried to outbid us, no one has succeeded in all these years. *Jay's* continues to enjoy an excellent reputation in Los Angeles County's South Bay area and at Carson Community Center. Recently, the city added another 15,000 square-foot wing to the center, and it is not unusual for us to serve over 1,200 people at one time. Sometimes, even I am amazed at our efficiency!

In the next few years, with the Olympics behind us and Carson a constant source of income, trouble began to brew. *Jay's Catering* was located in a commercial zone, adjacent to a residential one. Our trucks came in and out of a driveway at all hours, and since our building backed up to the residential area, the neighbors were not happy about the noise. I do not blame them but could not find a solution to the problem. People complained to the city council about the noise, and our reputation began to suffer. After some investigating, the problem was resolved. The city offered to buy the building and pointed us towards another one not far away. It turned out to be a blessing because it gave us an opportunity to grow again. Instead of occupying a mere 11,000 square foot building, we ended up in our present 36,000 square foot facility on a two-acre site in a Garden Grove Boulevard industrial complex.

> *...for riches certainly make themselves wings: they fly away as an eagle toward heaven.*
>
> —Pro. 23:5

16

Money In My Pocket Costs Me Plenty

With the proceeds from the sale of the Brookhurst Street building still in my pocket, I had the funds at my disposal when a man approached me about buying a lease on a Newport Beach waterfront building. This prime piece of real estate had two bayside docks adjacent to it. I envisioned great possibilities, using the building as a banquet facility and the docks for charter boats to load and unload passengers. Unlike me, my daughter Linda was not in favor of the purchase because she had an uneasy feeling about the deal. She protested the idea and said, "Dad, if you do this, I will quit." Well, in a few words, she dared me; I did, and she quit. Losing her was awful, but my real troubles were just beginning. After I had spent thousands of dollars on re-modeling the facility, the county of Orange informed me that I had no right to the docks. In the first place, they were not designed to hold big boats and secondly, for any boats that did dock, I would owe a royalty to the county! As you can imagine, I spent plenty in attorneys' fees, and in the end, lost a bundle of money. It appeared that my daughter was right.

I learned a big lesson that day. If you are in business with your children, do not make the mistake of failing to recognize when they have surpassed your level of competency. Children have a way of growing up and gaining experience that you might not have. By that time, my daughter was more qualified to run the business than I was, but I did not realize it. I thought I could do no wrong. Was I ever mistaken!

After Linda made good on her threat to leave, I called upon my sons to help manage *Jay's Catering*. John was 33 and Michael, who would assist him, was 28. John was instrumental in the growth of our company at that time particularly when he oversaw our move from Brookhurst Street to Garden Grove Boulevard. The City of Garden Grove had stipulated that we vacate the first building within 90 days or pay a $15,000 per month penalty. We faced the unbelievable task of gutting, designing and re-modeling our new facility as well as moving all our equipment out of the old, without closing down the business for one day. Weddings, parties, and banquets cannot wait.

John, with the help of my builder/friend Jim Stovall, immediately went to work on getting the new building ready for occupancy. Jim taught him the skills necessary to supervise the construction of a deluxe catering kitchen, reception area, office space, and attractive, new façade. John beat the odds and managed to finish the work in the allotted 90 days. We moved in right on time on April 1, 1987.

With construction out of the way, John turned his attention to other matters—like hiring his brother-in-law, Jeff Stevens, to computerize our entire system—from sales orders to food requisition. Jeff streamlined our procedures and put into effect methods we still use today. Jeff was named CEO of Jay's when John and his brother, Michael, left to run *Hole-n-One*, the golf tournament catering business they have owned for 16 years.

The longer we were in business, the more apparent each family member's strengths and talents became. My wife was the chief cook; I was the creative director/salesman; Linda was the Manager; Michael was an expert at serving as the lead on parties, and John, among other talents, found his initial niche in decorating. Salesmanship and management were skills he added later.

Under Helen Conti's direction, John learned everything he could about design and proceeded to create and build the sets we used for theme parties. He had several impressive sets made for my 60th birthday party, but the drawback was that it took us months to find a home for them after the party. John had a definite thirst for big, social events and loved getting those jobs for Jay's. Along with Helen, his wife Debbie, and Norman Myer, another designer who worked for us for nearly 10 years, John put us on the map when it came to doing large, elegant jobs in upscale neighborhoods. Once, he landed an open house in Laguna Hills for a construction company from England specializing in expensive homes. Their budget was $200,000, which today would translate into $350,000 to $400,000 for an open house!

From that point on, we began to get more social events and weddings in places like Laguna Beach and Huntington Harbor. John developed our business with boat parade participants (boat owners who decorate and celebrate on their boats and/or their waterfront homes over the holidays) in Huntington Harbor and Newport Beach. We catered 15 parties in Huntington Harbor one night and 10 or 12 in Newport Beach the next. They were a feather in our cap. Overall, John left his mark on *Jay's Catering.*

Former First Lady Barbara Bush, was a guest at a reception at the Newport Beach facility

John is married and the father of two girls, Alison and Alexandra. He and his wife Debbie moved to Fallbrook, Calif., in San Diego County, 75 miles from us about 10 years ago. They live in a 4,000 square foot mountaintop home with breathtaking views to the east and to the south. In the tradition of his grandfather, John tried his hand at raising avocados there for a time, but has since converted his avocado garden to a basketball/tennis court. Their daughter Alison graduated magna cum laude from Concordia University and will receive her master's degree from Azusa Pacific University in May 2007. She is a fifth grade teacher at a private school and worked her way through college as a behavioral therapist for autistic children. Alison wed Tim James in 2003 in Fallbrook. John and Debbie's backyard was transformed into a wonderland setting for the reception, thanks to the efforts of family, friends and Jay's Catering. Since marrying, the young couple has continued to pursue their love for traveling as well as a love for snowboarding, which has taken them all over North America on yearly trips with both of their families. At this time, Alison is expecting our first great grandchild!

Alexandra, their second daughter, has always been my "Candy Girl." She has been able to sniff out candy since she was two! Alexandra had a natural talent for gymnastics and amazed us all with her abilities. Throughout her school years, she also enjoyed dancing, performing arts, and singing. She is enrolled at the University of Colorado at Boulder, where she is pursuing a career as a criminal profiler and studying French. In Colorado, she enjoys snow skiing. Alexandra loves to travel and has been to Europe several times, as well as to Hong Kong and Australia. Both girls have enjoyed the opportunity to work parties for Jay's Catering in the past.

John's wife of more than 20 years, Debbie, works at Jay's Catering as a decorator when she is not assisting her husband with *Hole-n-One*. As a couple, they remind me of my wife and me. Debbie is a terrific wife as well as the perfect business companion for my son. She writes up the proposals and provides office support while John travels to present the bids and oversee operations once the golf tournament is under way. The two of them work very well together.

John with Debbie, Alison and Alexandra

The father of the righteous shall greatly rejoice: and he that begets a wise child shall have joy of him.

—Pro. 23:24

17

Hole-N-One

In 1989, *Jay's Catering* bid on an LPGA tournament that was coming to Orange County in nearby Buena Park. We had never catered a golf tournament before but decided to bid on it anyway. Amazingly, we were the successful bidder, but then faced the problem of how to feed a large number of people, who would pay us in cash—something to which we were not accustomed. For the first tournament, we opted for a belly-up concept, where patrons placed their orders at several windows. We were not pleased with the way that worked, so we adopted a system we originally used when I had handled food service for the school districts earlier. I developed a system where customers proceeded down either side of a food line, and paid the attendant at the end. We used the speed-line concept at the following golf tournaments, and it proved expeditious in getting people fed much quicker. With the speed-line concept, you can feed five people for every one served by the belly-up method in the same amount of time.

A few of the organizers from the Los Angeles Open were in attendance at the LPGA tournament, and we struck up a conversation. They must have been impressed because they offered us the chance to cater the LA Open in 1991. The LA Open plays host to over 50,000 people in a five-day period. It brought in $400,000 worth of business the first year.

My sons were so excited about golf tournaments that they encouraged me to go after more of the same business. To hear Michael tell it, "After the first classic in 1989, we bid on Greg Norman's "Shark Shootout" in November at the Sherwood Country Club in Los Angeles County, 65 miles north of our home base. We lost the bid to a San Francisco-based company. It just so happened that San Francisco suffered an earthquake in October of that year, and the winning bidder had to back out of the contract. *International Management Group*, or IMG, then asked if we would like to manage the concession stands. Although we had only one-month's notice, we said "yes," and pulled it off to their satisfaction. IMG is a billion dollar company that manages sports figures like Greg Norman and Tiger Woods. The next year, they again awarded us the concession for the Shark Shootout, as well as jobs in Utah and Minnesota. In 1989, we did two tournaments; in 1990, we did five; and in 1991, we did eleven. By 1995, we were up to 23 jobs and on the road eight months out of the year. Strange as it may seem, we owe our start and fortune to the San Francisco Earthquake of 1989! That is how we began our association with IMG and have now catered golf tournaments in 20 states, as well as Canada, because of them."

A few years after the LA Open, I noticed that John and Mike were spending more and more time on the golf tournaments, and less and less time on the business at hand, namely our regular catered events. I got the bright idea that we should start a separate corporation, allowing the boys to go into the golf tournament business full time and develop something for themselves. They thought it was a great idea, and we harmoniously split off *Hole-n-One* from *Jay's Catering*. It became a partnership within a partnership, and I arranged a sweetheart deal, whereby they would pay *Jay's Catering* $100,000 for a portion of our business, which was bringing in $700,000 easily.

Hole-n-One on site

When we started, we had none of the necessary equipment and needed to rent everything. Today, *Hole-n-One* is self-sustaining and owns all its equipment. Michael relates the story of their first tournament in Canada. "It was an extremely big job for a brand new tournament. John, our advance man, reported that the job was too difficult for us to attempt. I disagreed and felt sure we could manage if we were prepared well in advance. Fortunately, we won the bid and arrived nine days early to begin setup. This tournament involved serving food in almost 80 different locations, and required 250 locals, plus 25 staff members from California, as well as the challenge of clearing customs with personnel and equipment. In the end, the Canadian tournament rang up sales of $1.2 million!"

From that experience, John and Michael decided it was better to seek out the larger, more profitable tournaments. By eliminating at least four smaller ones, my sons could spend less time on the road and more time with their families.

The next year, they serviced another huge tournament, the International, in Colorado, and again eliminated several less profitable ones. By concentrating on the big tourneys, *Hole-n-One* now provides concession and hospitality for twelve or thirteen a year, down from a high of 23. Michael remembers when they once spent 47 consecutive days on the road, catering five jobs in seven weeks, and described it as "pure hell."

Putting on one of these tournaments is very difficult under the best of circumstances, let alone when you are 3,000 miles from home. It is amazing, but somehow they manage it. It takes four to five days to set up the concessions once the 54-foot trailers, hauled by a trucking company, arrive with supplies. These trailers house a virtual mobile kitchen, complete with a linoleum floor that meets health department standards, stoves, refrigerators, chairs, tables, 10 x 10 canopies and eight golf carts used to get around the courses! In every city, a large food purveyor is contracted to bring in a refrigerated truck full of groceries to the site, and deliver more whenever necessary. The company sponsoring the tournament, usually Coca-Cola or PepsiCo, provides full truckloads of inventoried beverages. Two or three chefs from Jay's Catering make the trip to the tournament and prepare hot foods for the concession stands as well as the lunches and dinners served in the hospitality tents. About 20 to 25 husband and wife teams of golf enthusiasts/travelers drive their motor homes to the tournaments to serve as concession workers. Some of these individuals have been with the company since the LA Open. When a team decides to retire, it finds its own replacement, since the job is a fun and lucrative one, given the heavy tipping that goes on at golf tournaments!

As of this writing, John is working in Florida, the new home of the Greg Norman Shark Tournament. *Hole-n-One* still provides food and concession at the Sherwood Country Club during the Tiger Woods Shootout, and recently celebrated 17 years as the official caterer of the LA Open. After 16 years, both John and Michael are beginning to tire and have expressed a desire to quit traveling. Still on the Board of Directors at Jay's, John and Michael run their businesses with the help of their wives, Debbie and Theresa. I have never heard of a problem between them or their wives. In fact, the two couples took a trip to Europe together for 17 days this past summer—a first for them considering they are usually too busy to take an extended vacation so far from home.

I sometimes wonder if I did the wrong thing in persuading John and Mike to go out on their own. If I had not sold them *Hole-n-One*, we may or may not have endured turmoil in the family as my children positioned themselves for leadership. A lot of the time, family members in business do have difficulty getting along. If I had to do it all over again, I probably would not have spun off a second business for my sons. I would have worked to keep us united and tried to give everyone an opportunity to develop a position in which each felt he worked best.

Instead of thy fathers shall be thy children, whom thou mayest make princes in all the earth.

—Psalm 45:16

18

Passing On The Dream

I wish my father were alive to see how my son, Michael, and his family have accomplished the vision that he spoke to me about often. My father's dream was that his children would do better than he did, and his grandkids would do better than their parents would. He wanted us to go into a family business so we could work and succeed together. If he could see Michael now, he would realize that his dream has come true. Michael, who has worked since he was about eight years old, is now 45. As a kid, he used to sweep the driveway at our Midway City location. Later on, he helped me deliver the lunches for Mercury Savings and food for parties, and, as a teenager, worked weddings and parties as the lead server. He also managed our Carson facility for its first six months in operation. Outside of the business and school, Michael had little time to pursue his passion—sports—but somehow found enough time to play and watch basketball, baseball and football. Although he had natural talent, he lacked the necessary height and build. Working for the family did not allow him to excel in sports as he would have liked.

Nevertheless, employment with us did have its advantages. It was at work one Saturday afternoon that Michael met his wife, Theresa, when she came to arrange for a wedding. Michael was the salesman who wrote up her order. Smitten from the moment she walked in, he could not take his eyes off her. However, he was under the impression she was getting married—that is, until she came back a week later to finalize plans with her sister, who it turns out, was the real bride-to-be. He was delighted and asked Theresa for a date. They began dating and got married themselves shortly thereafter. They reside in Orange, Calif., in a beautiful home that Theresa decorated. Interior design happens to be her passion, and she is in college working toward a degree.

When Michael's three sons came along, he encouraged them to play any sport they wanted, and even coached many of their Little League baseball and Pop Warner football teams. A good education was important to Michael and Theresa, so they sent all three boys to private elementary school. Each one graduated from Mater Dei High School, one of southern California's premier schools for both academics and sports. Like most parents, Michael wanted to give his children everything and worked tirelessly to support them. While he traveled for his business, Theresa stayed home and made sure they did their homework and got to their practices and games. She was concerned about their well-being, their upbringing, and their behavior. When he was in town, Michael went to as many of their ball games as possible—sometimes watching games all day long—just to make sure he spent equal time with his three sons. One of the greatest joys of his life was being there to watch Michael Jr., Nick, and Vince play football, baseball, basketball, and water polo.

Michael's obsession with sports never ended. His livelihood for the past 16 years has allowed him to "live" on golf courses around the country—albeit, providing food service, not golfing. He has recently ventured into another business, *American Sports Center* in Anaheim, just a few miles from Disneyland. Michael has found his niche in providing food service in a venue where sports teams compete in volleyball and basketball tournaments on weekends. He personally designed the kitchen and dining area, which seats 160 people. On a good day, the snack bar serves 2,500 people from a menu that includes traditional snack foods as well as teriyaki chicken rice bowls, the most requested item. Recently, he added a coffee, juice and smoothie bar that is doing an incredible amount of business. Sometimes, as many as 50 or 60 people wait in line for the smoothies that five blenders are making as quickly as possible. They call my youngest child "Big Mike" because of his big heart, and I could not be prouder.

I might remind you that my father, Giovanni, could not speak or write a word of English when he came to this country. He was uneducated and could not even tell time. I graduated from the eighth grade, and my three children, Linda, John, and Michael, graduated from high school before they entered the family business. Michael's three sons either are college graduates or will soon be. Michael Jr., their first child, graduated magna cum laude from Clemson University in Clemson, South Carolina, in 2006. While at Clemson, he met his wife, Jenny, who graduated summa cum laude at the same time. He works as an engineer, and she is pursuing a master's degree at the University of California in Irvine. Nick Mastroianni, their second son, is a senior at USC's Marshall School of Business, where he has been on the dean's list twice and already has a job lined up. Vince Mastroianni, the youngest, is currently enrolled at San Diego State University majoring in Real Estate Development. Mike's three sons have all traveled to Europe more than once, and each drives a nice car, thanks to the hard work of their father.

I think my father, their great grandfather, would be proud to know that his offspring are well-educated and living the American dream. Interestingly enough, it has taken only a generation for my father's dream to come true, and I am certain I have exceeded his expectations.

Michael, Vince and Nick Mastroianni

Vince, Michael Sr., Jenny, Michael, Teresa and Nick Mastroianni

I have played the fool,
and erred exceedingly.

—1 Sam. 26:21b

19

Father Doesn't Always Know Best

It was late in 1986 when my daughter Linda left *Jay's Catering*. With her no longer involved in the day-to-day operations, I began to make some major errors and continued to do so until her return in 1994. These blunders included going into partnership with a limousine company, taking over and fixing up a facility in Yorba Linda that turned out to be a dud, buying a seat on the board of a local bank, which went out of business within a year, and suffering a major loss with a cruise ship company.

In looking back, I believe I lost money in the limousine business because the personal computer era had not arrived in the early 1980s. Limousine service flourished after the advent of the personal computer when individuals could dial up the internet, search for a limousine service anywhere in the country, call direct to a central location and retain a limo, no matter where they lived. We were not fortunate enough to have the World Wide Web as a way of getting customers in those days. It was much more difficult. Had I hung on, we might be in business today, but the limo business is still a tough business—especially the competitive, airport runs. Although we charged $100 for a trip to the airport, we still lost money.

As for Yorba Linda—I leased a 10,000 square-foot office structure in an upscale area, conducive for business functions during the week and weddings and banquets on weekends. I invested $100,000 to remodel it, but did not have an effective way of marketing it to customers. Again, with the help of the World Wide Web, we might have been able to make a success of it. Today, at Jay's Catering, we get 3,500 hits per month on our website!

I learned another expensive lesson when I agreed to run the concessions for *Catalina Cruise Lines* about twenty years ago. They operated several 100-foot ships out of San Pedro and Long Beach, Calif., making daily round trips to Catalina Island. We collected $200,000 or more a month in the summer, and of course, less in the winter. A Brinks truck was dispatched to the docks every Monday morning to pick up the money. One weekend, along with my son-in-law, his brother, and my son, Michael, I went to Mexico to visit the elder Barragans and left an employee in charge. A native of South America, the man was responsible for loading the food onto the ships and keeping the inventory. Upon our return, the *Brinks Company* informed us that instead of the $45,000 that was supposed to be in the bag that Monday morning, there was nothing but crumbled-up newspaper. My man-in-charge was long gone and I felt there was no chance of finding him since he had probably headed back to his native country. He was not a bonded employee, so my insurance company did not cover my loss. Losing $45,000 would not have stopped me from continuing, but a short time later, a competitor with faster boats took away all of Catalina Cruises' business, and we were out of a contract.

Linda runs Jay's today

For all his days are sorrowful, and his work burdensome: even in the night his heart takes no rest.

—Ecc. 2:23

20

Los Caballeros

When an opportunity presented itself, I bid on and won the food concessions at *Los Caballeros Sports Club* in Fountain Valley in 1989. In addition to condominiums, apartments, a pool and gym, "Los Cab" sported a bar, restaurant area and banquet facility on premise. Shortly before getting involved at "Los Cab," my wife and I had decided to let our sons run *Jay's Catering*, and had gone into a self-imposed exile. I was feeling "low" due to my numerous bad investments and needed something to pick myself up out of a depression. Los Caballeros provided the impetus. I named the bar *Half Time*, the Italian restaurant, *Ciao Bella*, and rented out the upstairs as banquet facilities in order to bring in more revenue.

I was there night and day. At my age, it was a little embarrassing. *Ciao Bella* only represented 20 per cent of our businesses, but 90 percent of our time. It did not make sense, but I never gave up trying. If I did anything in my life that was successful due to my efforts, with Eleanor's constant support, *Ciao Bella* was it. We finally had a popular Italian restaurant, serving a steady clientele, so I hired an Italian singer and his three-piece band. The band, providing entertainment on Saturdays and Sunday nights, brought in people who liked Italian music, but caused others, who preferred only Italian food, not to stick around. At an expense of $300 a night, we failed to increase business, so we had to do away with the musicians.

While getting "Los Cab" going, I hired three different salespeople to assist me in selling banquets. None of them worked out, until a young woman, named Cynthia Shofner, came to work for me in 1991. Cynthia was so good that I gradually let the other three girls go, one by one. Although Cynthia started as a receptionist at $6 an hour, she became my "right hand man," literally and figuratively. Since I had lost the use of my right arm and was not left-handed, I relied on Cynthia to do all the typing, paperwork and eventually, the selling. She excelled at her job, signing up banquet after banquet after banquet. Together, we developed a good rapport, and between the bar, the restaurant and the banquet facility, were so successful that we had to hire another chef, in addition to the two Italian chefs we already had. One of them introduced me to Abdul Eldeib, an executive chef whom I quickly hired. Abdul just celebrated 17 years in our employ, but more about him later.

I will not ever forget Cynthia because I gave her a break when she needed it and she never forgot it. My wife and I realized that we had an employee who was very important to our operation, and we wanted to do anything we could to help her. That is why we bought her a 25" color television when we learned she had none. Cynthia says that our kindness and generosity resulted in a turning point in her life. For the past twelve years, she has served as the Sales Manager at the 100,000-square foot banquet facility we operate in the Carson Community Center. She has honored me by remaining a loyal employee all these years and has done an exceptional job.

Jay, Executive Chef Abdul and Dominico, the maitre'd

Jay in the Ciao Bella dining room

"Therefore I went about to cause my heart to despair of all the labour which I took under the sun."

—Ecc. 2:20

21

Out Of Commission

Overall, I squandered about a million dollars in two years. In 1992, I got myself into more trouble. I thought that branching out into the corporate feeding program would be a natural extension of our business. We took over cafeteria operations at two Nissan office buildings in Carson, and at the *Bank of America* district offices in Orange, Calif. The idea was a good one, but I quickly realized we had a major problem with cash control. Theft and pilfering became overwhelming issues. Although customers loved our food and the companies loved me, running these satellite operations did not work for us. In addition, I purchased and placed 24 vending machines in the three cafeterias, and they, too, quickly became a source of aggravation due to problems with money collection and security.

To make matters worse, I suffered a heart attack and had to have open-heart surgery. There was no one in the company to provide backup for these pilot programs that I was supervising on a daily basis. I was out of commission for the next six months, thanks to two more surgeries. My son John had his hands full running *Jay's Catering* and did not need the added stress of the cafeterias. While I was in the hospital, a frustrated John decided to rid the company of these "side" businesses, and I was glad he did.

I was beginning to think that my Midas touch had worn off. Now, nothing I touched turned to gold. In fact, in the preceding six years, between 1986 and 1992, I had nearly destroyed everything my family had worked so hard to accomplish. My daughter and I were civil to each other during this time as long as we did not discuss business. Our relationship improved and we became a little closer.

In fact, her daughter Christy was the reason for much of our contact. Many of the grandkids were involved in youth sports, but my granddaughter Christy took her love of sports to a higher level. In high school, Christy played softball as well as basketball and led her Calvary Chapel High School team to two state softball championships. Her high school career as a softball player was so illustrious that her school retired her number, 34, and her uniform still hangs in the gym to this day. She attended University of Oklahoma on a full softball scholarship, and in her junior year, her team won the NCAA Women's Softball College World Series. A picture of her with President George Bush hangs in my office, compliments of the day her winning team was invited to the White House.

My wife and I loved to go to Christy's games. In fact, we saw most of them, including many "away" games. One weekend, along with Linda's three other children, we flew to Miami to watch Christy play ball. Christy was known as a bunter and a solid extra base hitter. She had never hit a homerun, but that day, she did. After the game, she came over to me and said, "I hit one for my grandma and grandpa!" I will never forget it.

President George W. Bush with Christy Ring, my granddaughter

"Wherefore I perceive that there is nothing better than a man should rejoice in his own works; for that is his portion: for who shall bring him to see what shall be after him?"

—Ecc. 3:22

22

Invest In Yourself

I BEGAN TO REALIZE that I could no longer handle Los Caballeros because it was too much work for me. At about the same time, my daughter Linda moved the base of operations for her catering business, *Chiappe's*, to Los Caballeros. Eventually, we closed *Ciao Bella*, and in 1994, she decided to come back to our family business as well. It did not happen soon enough. She threw herself in to her job with a renewed zeal, and won the respect of all our employees. From that point on, the tide began to turn.

For the record, I have not made an outside investment in 15 years. Previously, I invested in other projects or ideas believing I would make money, but most of the time, I did not. In fact, every investment—whether a stock, bank, or banquet hall—turned out to be a loser, with the exception of real estate. I have never owned a piece of property that did not appreciate in value. Every one of my real estate investments has turned a profit, and several of them made me a great deal of money.

As far as *Jay's Catering* is concerned, it has been profitable for the last 15 years. With profits, we re-invest in the company. For example, this past year, we spent $25,000 on a barbecue oven, and re-modeled our building façade and portions of the interior.

My advice is to invest in your own company or dreams, instead of someone else's. You can control your money and decide how best to use it. Why let someone else play with your hard-earned cash?

> *Many daughters have done virtuously, but thou excellent them all.*
>
> —Pro. 31:29

23

Under New Management

Since my "retirement," my daughter has been busy building a financially viable and efficiently run catering powerhouse. When she returned from a seven-year hiatus, our cash reserves were only $16,000, and we were heavily in debt. In the ensuing years, she has never borrowed a penny for operating expenses and has retired the large debt she inherited. When she came back, we owned 12 vehicles. Today, we have a fleet of 33, all paid in full. She has implemented uniforms for our kitchen, warehouse, delivery, and serving personnel, and installed proper shelving and re-organized the warehouse to make better use of space to house our equipment. Thanks to Linda, the sales staff works on a commission pay system in newly-remodeled offices.

Linda maintains good relations with our customers as well as our employees. She takes a personal interest in them and they are comfortable under her direction. Some comment that she rules with "an iron fist in a silk glove." Nevertheless, she has earned their love and respect. The proof is in the longevity of our people—many of whom have been with us for twenty or more years. Linda has surrounded herself with a strong management team and gives them the freedom to run their own departments as they see fit. She also pampers employees with company parties, picnics, baseball games and a spa day, but never feels she does enough for them.

Words are insufficient to praise my daughter, who started working with us when she was only 15. She is a keen executive with great instincts that I trust unequivocally. My wife and I can rest comfortably at night knowing that such a capable, competent woman is at the helm of the company we started. As I mentioned earlier, my biggest problem with Linda was not accepting the fact that she had grown up. I saw myself as her father, and expected her to listen to me, not realizing that she was more astute in business than I was. I created more problems for her after my unofficial/official retirement because I could not keep my nose out of the business and continued to try to get her to listen to my ideas, which she rightly rejected. I kept butting in and making her angry. Although I busied myself with projects, this sympathetic old man who had had a nice career, did not have the sense to go away. The difference between my daughter and me is that I led by the "yell, scream, and cuss system" while mild-mannered Linda has a better leadership style. The employees respond well to both of us, but her way is best.

On a personal note, Linda is married to Uriel Loaeza, our Operations Manager and the individual responsible for routing our deliveries, buying products, liquor, and beverages, controlling labor costs, and monitoring the back end of our facility—where products enter and leave the building. Uriel is tireless, industrious, enterprising and a great asset to this organization. Together, he and Linda have a six-year-old son, Jacob, whom they both adore, and are raising Uriel Jr., his 17-year-old son from a previous marriage, a budding chef who recently won a contest for high school chefs and a $5,000 scholarship to the Art Institute of California in Orange County. Linda's two older children, Michael Ring and Christy Ring, are working adults. Michael is married to Gina and employed at Jay's, and Christy works as a private batting coach. Linda's two younger sons, Brian and AJ, are still in school—Brian, at USC's Marshall School of Business in Los Angeles, and AJ, at Calvary Chapel High School in Costa Mesa, Calif. Brian has been a hard-working, intelligent individual with a lifelong love for all sports. He received a partial scholarship to USC and was salutatorian of his high school class. His younger brother AJ is one of the nicest and funniest kids I have ever known. He, too, is an athlete (golf and basketball), editor of his high school yearbook and recently traveled to Brazil on a missionary trip with his pastors.

"Providing for honest things, not only in the sight of the Lord, but also in the sight of men."

—2 Cor. 8:21

24

My Formula For Selling

Learning how to spend your money competently is second only in importance to making the money in the first place. As a salesman, I always felt I was a professional salesman, who was a nobody. Sometimes, you can be a nobody, with little or no education, and still be effective and have the ability to sell. In fact, I worked out a formula for selling that I perfected over the years. I practiced and practiced and practiced it. To me, it was simple because I had created it myself. I did not get it from a book. I learned it in the school of hard knocks. This formula was part of me—it was me. You could call it my mission statement. This is it:

1. Be Honest
2. Be Yourself
3. Be Sincere
4. Have a good knowledge of the product you are selling. Convince others that you know your product well and the customer will have confidence in you.
5. Instill in them a trust of you. Once you gain their trust, you have the sale. I don't care who the competition is.
6. Convince them that you want their business.

7. Most importantly, get them to like you. Unless they like you, they will not give you their business.

We also live by three important commitments when it comes to our food. We believe that:

1. If you can't bake it, cook it, or make it, then don't do it.
2. Never offer a menu unless the prices are included.
3. Make sure everything is fresh.

To me, this became the foundation of our catering business and I thank my family for sticking to these goals for the last 35 years.

Michael, Linda, John, Jay & Eleanor

For a dream comes through the multitude of business.

—Ecc. 5:3

25

It's a Good Thing I Am The Boss

(That's all I know how to be!)

I HAVE ALWAYS BEEN A DREAMER, and when you are in business, you dream up ideas to implement in the morning. I cannot be a receptionist, accountant, cook, or warehouse manager, but I can dream up incredible ideas in the middle of the night. I think of myself as the company dreamer. That is what I do best.

Besides dreaming, I watch the numbers. I keep abreast of sales, receipts, and bank statements on a daily basis. I am aware of our financial condition at all times—making sure everything is on track.

Another job I hold is that of official taste-tester. I have been tasting food since my wife made her first lasagna years ago, and I suggested how to improve it. Since then I have set the standards for over a hundred different items we now offer on our menus. I have always believed that it is better to serve the very best hamburger than to serve a cheap steak. I learned that early on.

When I delivered to the hospitals on my milk route, I observed how the kitchens operated and noticed the ingredients they were using in their cooking. I realized that the kitchen staff was not preparing meals but merely re-heating frozen food. The hospitals thought they were keeping costs down by employing fewer cooks, but I believe it cost them more. For instance, it costs 40 cents to buy a cupcake, but only 10 cents to make one. You can bake 800 rolls for 3 cents each in less than a half hour, but it will cost 15 cents apiece to buy them. Many restaurants and hospitals have a variety of portion-controlled items available to them, so they put a meal together with these items rather than make meals from scratch. The result is not nearly as good.

I told myself that if I ever went into business for myself, I certainly would not operate that way. I recalled my father's philosophy, "If you make it yourself, it's cheaper and better." I believed that philosophy and hoped to implement it on a consistent basis. I also vowed never to buy anything that was ready-made or frozen. If you have the volume and are able to make everything yourself, you come out ahead. You will have a good product that people like better and save money, besides. From day One, we made everything fresh in our kitchen, including potato and macaroni salads, lasagna, and meatballs. We baked our own bread, rolls, cakes, cookies, and pastries on a daily basis. When buying from a commercial bakery, you only get fresh items four days a week since there are generally no deliveries on Wednesday. There is a good chance that your Thursday delivery could be leftovers from Tuesday and at least two days old!

The "one-stop shopping" concept came to my attention many years ago as I drove my catering trucks to the construction sites. There was a company advertising "one-stop shopping," and the idea stuck with me. I decided to incorporate it into the catering business. We would offer everything under one roof—from food, beverages, cakes, and flowers, to tables, chairs, linens and other rental items. We would also recommend reception halls, photographers, and musicians. To my knowledge, there was not another caterer like that in Orange County, Calif., and to this day, there still is not. An interesting fact is that even though we are one of the largest and best caterers, we only capture less than 1 percent of the business. I have no way to prove this statistic, but it is based on the assumption that in a county of three million people, there are possibly 10,000 events going on daily, and we cater 100 parties on our best days; thus we are catering less than 1 percent of the events. Most caterers are individuals or of the "mom and pop" variety, which is what my wife and I were when we started.

From the beginning, we ran our kitchen like an efficient factory and employed techniques similar to other factories. Each department—e.g., sales, rentals, linens, cake and beverage—provides a different function. After a salesperson takes an order, he or she gives the work orders to the departments involved. Every department gets a separate order and fills it. On the day of the event, the department sends its completed order to the dock for delivery to the customer. Most factories operate in a comparable fashion.

After the sale, the kitchen manager takes on the responsibility of getting the job done. He assembles all the orders and decides on the amounts of food necessary to fill them. For example, he might need six pans of lasagna, 12 pans of chicken cacciatore, and 1800 rolls. He places the work orders on the kitchen board in order of the time they are leaving the building the next day. This production list is done by 5 p.m. so the night shift can do the cooking, baking and preparation work. Obviously, supplies from the other departments are added to the food order, and then the entire order is picked up by or delivered to the customer. This simple process has worked wonderfully for us for years.

I got the idea of being able to fill last-minute orders from a flower shop at the corner of 17th St. and Bristol in Santa Ana, Calif. The owner always had a large array of beautiful arrangements outside his shop. One day, I asked him why he made up the bouquets in advance. He informed me that people like to walk in and pick up flowers at the last minute. "Many customers do not have the luxury of ordering in advance, so I have the flowers ready. My customers appreciate that, and consequently, I do a high volume of business," he said. I liked that philosophy and decided to incorporate it into my business. If a customer places an order by 2 p.m., he or she can pick it up or have it delivered the next day. This policy offers the same thing as my friend's flower shop: prompt service on last-minute orders.

This last-minute policy has allowed us to develop a working relationship with a large utility company. Any time there is a major fire in Orange or San Bernardino counties, they call us to feed their workers. Without much advance notice, we can give them whatever they need.

In addition, between 9 a.m. and 2 p.m. on any given day, we get as many as 20 orders for the next day. It amounts to quite a lot of business, and we profit nicely. Besides, our customers depend on us. Many a secretary has been asked by her boss to arrange for a breakfast meeting the next day. She calls us by 2 p.m. to place her order, and we can accommodate her request.

For I know the thoughts that I think toward you, sayeth the Lord, thoughts of peace, and not of evil, to give you an expected end.

—Jer. 29:11

26

Creative Genius

Despite what some would say are very serious handicaps, I started a family-owned business that did $12 million worth of business last year. Simply put, I cannot read. Today, I might be called "learning disabled." I am not certain of the reason, but several factors could have contributed to the fact that I never learned to read properly. For instance, I grew up in an English-speaking country with Italian-speaking parents, who moved around a lot. By ninth grade, I knew I could not read, and that is what prompted me to drop out of school.

I have never read a book in my life. It would take me ten minutes just to read one page, and that is too slow for it to make any sense. Consequently, I have had to depend upon my wife or another family or staff member to help me understand the written word. Yet, I do not believe anyone ever caught on. Fortunately, my style of doing business has been of a more personal nature. "Make friends first, do business next" has really worked for me. I brought in the clients and my family and staff took care of the paper work.

At 77 years old, I now realize that being a poor reader and a ninth grade dropout has forced me to develop something else—a sixth sense, more or less. I have had to rely on this "something else" to get by. I did not have the luxury of reading books to discover how other people did things, so I invented my own methods. Everything I did, from selling to designing or implementing ideas, has been rather unique and not at all traditional. One such invention was the "chef caddy." When we started doing a lot of corporate catering, it was difficult because there was no way to keep hot food hot and cold food cold, other than to deliver the food to the companies immediately after it was prepared. That was not easy. I began thinking about a chafing dish and the pan that goes inside it to keep the food warm. I realized that I needed to develop one container that could not only keep food warm, but also cold. Polypropylene came to mind, and I worked with a company to design the mold and produce the container. That company continues to make and sell my creation on the open market, and I receive a royalty. We personally use 4,000 "chef caddies" a month.

The first 25 years of my career, I operated in the expected manner—saying "Please" "Thank you", "Yes, sir" and " No, sir" when I walked into a person's office. Today, I might say, "Man, are you ugly!"—smiling all the while. I have used that line on people for the last 25 years, and they always laugh. I approach someone in a restaurant and say, "Are you going to eat all that? If not, save me some." Invariably, I get a laugh. One day, a woman took me seriously enough to bring me her doggie bag as she was leaving the restaurant. When I see a particular man on the janitorial staff at one of our facilities, I say, "Better get out of my way or I'll whip you." He laughs because he is much bigger than I am. I have found that humor opens the lines of communication.

If I had my "druthers," I would rather be well educated and do everything across the board the way it should be done. Since that is not the case, I have learned to appreciate my situation and make the best of it.

Secondly, I was diagnosed with bi-polar disorder some years ago after I went to see a doctor about what I thought was a serious illness. At the time, I could not carry a cup of coffee without shaking and was experiencing speech problems. I stuttered. It was very embarrassing. The doctor put me on Lithium and Depakote and adjusted the medication a few months later. With the proper medication, we seem to have resolved the problem. Once known as manic-depression, this mental disorder is characterized by extreme mood swings. My family can attest to the fact that I do experience mood swings, given the business risks I have taken when experiencing a "high" state of mind. I thought it was something bad when told I was bi-polar, but I now realize that I am at my creative best during those "up" moods. For many years, Jerry Kobrin, a local newspaper columnist referred to me as the "czar of catering,"—quite a compliment for someone like me. When I think of my accomplishments, and all the challenges I faced in this business, it is amazing what I have been able to do, given my eighth-grade education and other limitations. I went into the catering business without much forethought or planning. The only thing that qualified me to be a caterer is because I said I was one. Still, I came up with simple but quality menus as well as practical solutions for feeding small and large groups of people. We handle every type of catering, from wedding receptions and everyday parties to corporate banquets and church dinners.

I still have very bad short-term memory. You can say every old person has memory loss, but mine is severe. The fact is my short-term memory has gotten worse, but my long-term memory is better. I had been writing these memoirs on my own, and my daughter was so impressed, she hired someone to help me. My daughter does not pay me too many compliments, but after she read some of this material, she thought it was very thorough and was amazed that I remembered everything I did.

On the other hand, I no longer have a driver's license. I studied the driver's manual for ten days and felt confident I would pass the written driver's test, but when I started to take the test, my mind went blank. I could only answer two or three questions before giving up and going home—without my driver's license. That is an example of my short-term memory failing me.

Jay's "Chef Caddy"

What I did not know until I started penning this book is that I am also an overachiever. I keep talking about my accomplishments and contributions to *Jay's Catering*, but without the support of my family, I would not have been able to do any of it. Ideas are worthless unless you can put them in to practice. My family knew just how to make my ideas work. Early in our marriage, it became apparent that I was a leader, and Eleanor, a follower. Whenever I wanted to do something, I did it. She went along with my ideas, but with hesitation. She never gave me her unconditional blessing; many times, I felt I was forcing her to do things she did not want to. The business caused a lot of friction in our marriage and created other problems because my wife and kids could not keep up with my never-ending and sometimes crazy ideas. Eleanor would get angry and say, "You're moving too quickly. Slow down. We can't implement your ideas so fast!" She put me in my place, and I would stop, sit back for a while, and bring the same subject up later. Our kids usually agreed with their mother, making matters worse. Then, I had to convince all of them to go along with my plans. They tried to reason with me, but if I did not get my way, I got angry. I would cool off, let time pass and start all over again. There was no stopping me! It must have been a total strain on my poor wife to put up with me all these years. Still, she and my daughter worked with me to put my ideas into effect. I could never have operated this business without their constant help and support.

My daughter Linda's fifth grade teacher once told me that she was an excellent student and capable of completing a whole project herself. How blessed am I to have her running this company? My wife had the cooking and food knowledge. My sons, when they worked with us, provided a great deal of manpower. So together, we are responsible for this business known as *Jay's Catering*, to which we added the corporate name, Mastroianni Family Enterprises, some years ago.

"In all labor, there is profit…"

—Pro. 14:23

27

The Kitchen —A 24-Hour Operation

THINKING "OUT OF THE BOX" helped me build our kitchen, which is not a traditional restaurant kitchen, but a catering kitchen with extra preparation tables. When my son John and I originally sketched the floor plan, I took a wild guess at how big the kitchen should be and decided 8,000 square feet sounded good. It appears I made the right decision because we have not had to increase the kitchen's size since we built it in 1987. Our building originally housed a 30,000 square foot supermarket, and we added 4,500 square feet to the front for a reception area and offices and a 1,500 square-foot tool room. We employ 15 salespeople, four auxiliary office personnel, an accounting staff of three, 22 people in the warehouse, and 60 employees in the kitchen.

Jay's kitchen, under the expert management of Abdul Eldieb, our executive chef, operates seven days a week, 24 hours a day. Abdul is a professional chef who came to us with an impressive record. He holds a diploma from the Culinary Arts Institute in Concord, France (1973), a BS in Chemistry from the University of Cairo, Egypt (1980), and a degree in food sciences from UCLA (1986). While in our employ, he continues to add to his expertise and recently completed a course on Asian cuisine at the Culinary Institute of America's campus in Napa, Calif., in 2006. For seventeen years, Abdul has excited us with his culinary innovations and outstanding menus. He does an amazing job of overseeing a large kitchen staff, the majority of which comes in at 6 p.m. and works until early morning. Well respected by the staff, Abdul has elevated the art of buying from our purveyors to a science and single-handedly reduced our food and labor costs to such a degree that it makes a tremendous difference in our bottom line.

Assisting Abdul with administrative kitchen duties is Hossam Elsayed, whom we call Sam. Seventeen years ago, I hired Sam as a waiter and banquet man for *Los Caballeros*. He did everything we asked of him and did it well. No question that this man is one of the nicest and most versatile employees we have ever had. He is efficient, organized, a great leader, and also can cook, work as a gourmet waiter, and prepare tableside specialties. At one time, he worked in our accounting department. Everyone in the kitchen, in fact, in the whole company, loves him. Along with Abdul, he has been a great asset to Jay's Catering.

Executive Chef Abdul Eldieb

Voted the "Number 1 Caterer" in Orange County four of the last five years by the Orange County Register, we are the only full service, in-house caterer around. On a given day, we might handle as many as 75 corporate deliveries, plus the orders for our Carson site and private events. We have never reached capacity but have done as many as 100 catering jobs in a day. This past Thanksgiving, we prepared 80 complete dinners for full-service, deliveries and pick-ups.

Our rental department, with 11 full-time employees, is self-sustaining. We rarely have to subcontract a rental item because we own every type rental imaginable. Our linen department consists of four full-timers, who wash and iron linens of every size and shape from an inventory that contains over 2,000 tablecloths and drapes. The number of serving personnel in Garden Grove is 75, although it jumps to 150 during Christmas, our busiest season. In Carson, we have two managers, three salespeople, and 50 serving personnel, bringing our total number of employees to 247.

We offer health benefits, 401K, and vacation pay to all our full-time employees, who get a one-week vacation after the first year and up to three weeks after 7 years. When we were still a small, growing company, we knew it was important to keep our employees happy, so we offered as many benefits as we could. In return, our retention rate is very high, due in part to our good pay and equally as good benefits. Besides, many employees enjoy working for a family business.

Take for instance, Helen Conti, our first decorator and longest-term employee at 34 years, who has been with us since 1973. She brought her daughter, Gehnel, into the business as a cake decorator and her niece Gloria, who became one of our top salespeople and worked for us for over 25 years until her recent retirement. My sister-in-law, Betty Flati, has always been an integral part of *Jay's Catering.* She started working with my wife and me in the kitchen in our early days and has since graduated to handling the front office, and working in our accounting department. In addition, our salespeople, Frances Bingman, Lynn Likens and Tamera Schulz, have been with us 30, 26 and 21 years respectively.

He that delicately brings up his servant from a child shall have him become his son at the length.

—Pro. 29:21

28

From Boys To Men

Forty years ago, one of my best milk accounts was a brosarro labor camp in Huntington Beach. There were several hundred Mexican or South Americans living in that camp. I sold them 700 pints of milk a day—one for everyone in the camp. When President Kennedy was in office, he put a stop to the program, which sent immigrants out to the farm fields to pick strawberries and other crops. His administration believed that Americans were being denied jobs, so the immigrants were banned from going to the fields to work. After that, the government would send trucks to downtown LA to pick up people to work in the strawberry patches, but no one wanted to do the backbreaking labor, and if they did, they only lasted half a day.

I became friends with Señor Barragan, who was a cook at the camp, and visited with him every morning when I delivered the milk. On rainy days, I would take some of the workers, including his sons, Luis and J orge, to work in my kitchen. Several of our workers were boys (age 16 and up) when then started and have been with *Jay's Catering* for 30 years now. Another 20 to 25 have been with us anywhere from ten to 30 years. Roberto Mota Garcia comes to mind. As Abdul's right hand man, he is in charge in Abdul's absence. Trustworthy, reliable, and well-liked by his co-workers, Roberto also is in great demand as a chef for Hole-n-One tournaments.

Many of these long-time employees own homes and have raised families in the community. Years ago, I used to sit with three or four of them in my backyard, pointing out a different object and teaching them how to say it in English. They wanted to learn to speak our language, and they did. They wanted to improve their lot in life, and they did.

For me, the connection to their community is a personal one. I now have three grandsons who are children of these immigrants. One of them, Brian, a freshmen majoring in business at USC, is Linda's son with her husband, Luis Barragan, my first employee. Brian's father started working for me in 1971. It only took six months for him to become kitchen manager. Luis, and a few others, had an entrepreneurial spirit and wanted to watch, learn and open businesses in their own neighborhoods. His five brothers, including Jorge, who worked as our kitchen manager for 17 years, Rafael, our pastry chef for 20 years, and Javier, our baker for about the same number of years, and two sisters came to work for us. Eventually, all his family members went into business for themselves. Jorge now owns two restaurants; Rafael left to open a restaurant of his own and the third brother, Javier, who turned out thousands of Jay's always-popular cheese rolls daily, left several years ago to open a bakery. I never held them back. I loved and cared for the Barragan family and wanted to see them get ahead.

Jorge and Luis Barragan with Jay- the early days

> "*...a man hath no better thing under the sun, than to eat, and to drink, and to be merry:*"
>
> —Pro. 29:21

29

Best Of The Best Parties

Some of the best parties we have ever catered were my own. On the occasions of my 50th, 60th, and 75th birthdays, as well as family weddings, we put on very remarkable and memorable affairs. We used these parties to incorporate everything we knew about catering, sparing no expense, and calling upon every resource available to us. For my 50th birthday, we invited 300 people to a buffet fit for a king. Dressed like the Godfather, I arrived at the Garden Grove Community Center in a limousine and proceeded to provide our guests with hours of entertainment, by singers, musicians, belly dancers, and even a Steve Martin impersonator. Twenty-seven years have gone by and people still talk about it!

Ten years later, on my 60th birthday, we entertained 400 people at the Carson Community Center. My wife and I not only arrived at, but also drove into the hall in a 1930 Cadillac limousine, which my partner and I had rebuilt and stretched. For dinner, we served a sit-down meal of osso buco, an Italian dish of braised veal shanks in white wine. A 12-piece band, playing on a specially-built stage, provided entertainment at the party, which sported an all black and white décor. *Joe's Garage*, an antique car showroom in Tustin, Calif., was the site of my 75th Birthday Party. This time, my wife and I arrived in a 1957 Thunderbird, accompanied by bodyguards, formidably played by my nephews. Three hundred fifty guests enjoyed a buffet of every type food imaginable, and for entertainment, we enlisted a professional dinner-theatre presentation of "Joey and Maria's Comedy Italian Wedding."

My son Mike's wedding, my grandson Michael's, my granddaughter Alison's, and those of a few nieces and nephews were also occasions when *Jay's Catering* had a chance to shine. We incorporated the best of everything that experience had taught us. Each one was better than the last, and all of them were special because we were able to treat our family to unforgettable occasions as we learned more and more about efficiency and perfection.

In 2003, we hosted a party at our home using the best china, flatware, and linen and satin tablecloths. We offered an outstanding menu, featuring gourmet food, and an open bar. For decorations, floral centerpieces costing $50 each as well as larger, more expensive floral arrangements graced the buffet tables. Eight servers waited on the guests, passing hors d' oeuvres, and serving their meals. Strolling musicians added a nice touch. It was, without a doubt, the most exquisite party I have ever thrown. The price of the party for 55 guests was almost $12,000. It was not a celebration, just people socializing, and perhaps, talking business. The people who came did not have anything in common—they were virtual strangers, but they all had a wonderful time. It was a "test party," for my convenience, so I knew what to recommend the next time a client came to me asking for "the best we had to offer."

I was reminded of how far we have come since the days of our $4.95 per person cold buffet. When I started catering parties or big events, I had no idea what I was trying to accomplish, but in the end, we have been able to satisfy every type of customer—from the discriminating gourmet, to the budget-conscious bride and groom.

We handle party planning in much the same way an architect designs your dream house. He discusses with you everything you want—from the type of front door to the flooring, from kitchen cabinets to kitchen tops, and from the number and size of the rooms to the color of paint in each. You discuss with him how much money you have budgeted for the project. With information in hand, you make decisions concerning every aspect of the proposed house.

Similarly, we sit with our clients to discuss what they want—down to the last detail. We question whether a customer wants paper dishes, Corelle, or fine china. We ask what type silverware they prefer, what kind and color of linens they like, what rentals they will need, and of course, what food they want served—filet mignon, USDA grade steak, prime steak, chicken or any of our numerous ethnic specialties. Will it be served buffet or sit down style? We discuss the pricing differences, so the customer can stay within his or her budget and minimize or expand it as they see fit. Each of these items varies in price and affects the bottom line. As the expert, we can make suggestions on what works and what does not, but the customer has the final say—much like the house builder who tells the architect what he wants, within reason.

The most exquisite party I have ever thrown

Jay's 60th Birthday

Jay's 50th Birthday and Grace Raso and Helen Conti

> *Give us help from trouble: for vain is the help of man.*
>
> —Psalm 108:12

30

Disasters —Some Averted, Some Not

In this business, plenty of catastrophes can happen. Being the experienced caterer we are today, we try to avert most of them, but that was not always the case. The biggest disaster I can remember was a picnic we catered for a large insurance company in Irvine, Calif., about 25 years ago for 4,000 people. We had never served that many people before, but I was sure we could do it. I always say that if you can build one house, you can build two, or four or six or more. Following my philosophy, we attempted to serve a traditional picnic fare of chicken and hamburgers, with side dishes and drinks, to this crowd of thousands, but failed to realize just how difficult it would be. First, we had a problem with the chicken, which we always pre-cook in our ovens before we get to the job, then finish on the grill at the site. For this event, our kitchen apparently failed to cook the chicken well enough beforehand, so it took longer than usual to finish the onsite grilling. The lines were extremely long, the temperature, 85 degrees, and the people, very impatient.

In addition, our person in charge decided to use beverage service dispensers instead of cans—a less expensive way to go. That proved to be a disaster. The dispensers could not accommodate the volume of people coming through the lines fast enough. I found myself heading to nearby grocery stores to buy thousands of cans of beverages, as well as bags of ice. I threw my purchases into the back of my pickup truck as fast as I could and rushed back to the picnic area to deliver drinks to a very thirsty crowd. Besides being very embarrassing, it was also costly. To compensate for the bad service, I returned $8,000 of the insurance company's money—about half the cost of the job.

The following incident falls under the category of "disaster-averted." Everything, including the cake, was set up for a wedding we were catering at the Garden Grove Community Center. I could not believe it when about five minutes before the wedding party and guests were to arrive, the cake fell over and landed on the floor! At *Jay's Catering* at that time, we had been making artificial wedding cakes for display purposes, and it just so happened that we had that very same cake in our window. I thought about that cake, and quickly drove the mile or so to *Jay's* to retrieve it and made it back to the hall before the reception started. Since the edible bottom cake layer was still intact, I transferred the top three layers of the artificial cake onto it. No one could tell the difference. When the bride arrived, I pulled her aside to tell her the good and bad news. The bad news was that her cake had dropped to the floor. The good news was that we had plenty of cake for everybody and would serve the slices from the kitchen. She took it well—much better than expected.

We prevented another near-catastrophe in 1994, the year Linda merged her company, *Chiappe's*, with *Jay's*. Along with her staff, she brought over several existing orders. The first few weeks were a challenge as her sales staff learned to use our custom catering software, which by the way had greatly improved the efficiency of our operation and was the first of its kind in the industry. Today, several companies now produce catering software exclusively.

On Saturday about noon, a client who had booked her party with *Chiappe's* called Tamera Schulz, our sales coordinator at *Jay's*, to see what time the staff was arriving for the wedding she was hosting for a couple from her church. Tamera put the woman on hold and literally screamed for help. Due to unfamiliarity with the computer program, someone had entered the wedding on the wrong date, and our calendar showed nothing for this particular Saturday. We learned that two hundred guests were arriving shortly for the wedding!

Everyone dropped what they were doing and pulled together to get ready for the wedding. Cooks came in to make enchiladas, while members of our sales staff mixed guacamole, sliced fruit and cut up tortillas to fry for chips. Our designer, Norman, made punch and gathered other essential items. We located available servers and sent others from an earlier job to the event site. Fortunately, our client had her own cake and rental items, so we mostly had to furnish the food and service. As a team, we were able to put together a full Mexican menu for 200 people in less than two hours! No one at the wedding knew about the date mistake and the reception went off without a hitch.

Recently, we had another case of a "wrong date," but this one was due to human failure rather than computer error. In 2005, a large local union scheduled their employee picnic for Saturday, October 12th. *Jay's* had a contract to serve its barbecued chicken to 1,000 guests at a vast, Long Beach park. At 9 a.m.,

October 5th, our salesperson, Lynn Likens, was enjoying a day off when our office called her to report that the union contact was trying to reach her. She returned his call, only to find that he was irate because *Jay's* workers had not shown up at the 7 a.m. appointed time. Lynn wanted to believe he was playing a practical joke, but he was serious about his complaint. She checked the contract, only to confirm that the picnic was scheduled for the following Saturday. After a heated exchange, the contact whimpered, "Did I not tell you that we had to change our date to today?" She replied, "No. Never!" At that point, he realized his mistake of failing to tell us although he had remembered to inform all the other vendors, who were thankfully at the park already.

He then pleaded with Lynn to do something, and she did. After contacting my daughter Linda, her immediate boss, who assured Lynn that *Jay's Catering* would provide the food and service for the picnic, Lynn told the client that we would take care of everything. Unfortunately, barbecued chicken was out of the question because we did not have enough on hand, but hamburgers and hot dogs were not a problem. Learning this, the client said, "Great. I don't care! Baloney sandwiches would be fine at this point!" Lynn said that it was like calling the troops to arms or preparing for an emergency rescue. All available personnel were called in to help and the mood was "high alert." There was so much to do, yet so little time. She attributes the ability to get everything done to the presence of a higher power that day and a staff that handled the crisis with incredible skill and competency, despite the fact that it was already a busy Saturday for us.

The salad department whipped out 25 fresh fruit platters in less than an hour while the warehouse crew, under my son-in-law Uriel Loaeza's direction, performed the fastest setup known to man at the picnic site. We managed to put together a picnic for 1,000 people only 3 hours and 45 minutes after the initial phone call and were ready to serve hamburgers and hot dogs a mere 45 minutes later than the planned meal time. Lynn and the others refer to it as the "Panic Picnic" that no one around here will soon forget.

Two occasions when I had to rely on my wife Eleanor's cooking expertise come to mind. In 1973, a satisfied customer returned, requesting that we serve a dinner party she was planning. She asked if we "did" Beef Wellington, and I said, "Sure." Then I went into the kitchen to ask my wife what it was. She said she did not know but would look it up in her recipe books. After a sample test, Eleanor fell confident we could prepare the dish, which is filet mignon wrapped in a puff pastry, and we did—much to the satisfaction of our customer. Next, a mother-of-the-bride scheduled us to cater her daughter's wedding, but required that we serve a family recipe known as arroz con pollo, a Puerto Rican dish of chicken and rice, with saffron, peas, and olives, in a tomato sauce base. As Eleanor was following the mother's recipe, she felt it did not have enough flavor, and doctored it up. I was somewhat worried about what our customer would say, but she returned to compliment us on the most fabulous arroz con pollo she had ever eaten. We talked about that incident for years.

For God gives to a man that is good in his sight wisdom, and knowledge and joy...

—Ecc. 2:26

31

Valuable Lessons Learned

Thirty years ago, as I struggled to figure out how to do more than one event at a time, I learned a valuable lesson. The first time we did two weddings on a Saturday, everything went well, and I gained lot of confidence. However, the next Saturday, we catered only one wedding, but we did only a fair to middling job. I found out that you have to concentrate on what you do. If you are not organized, things will not go as well. With only one wedding, we messed up, but with two, it was perfect. Consequently, we became better organized, using checklists and double-checking the food orders and supplies before they left our shop. We quickly went from three to four to five and six wedding receptions on a Saturday. Today, we average 15 or 20 on Saturdays during the traditional summer wedding season.

After establishing we could handle multiple events, I questioned the distance we could travel. Could we honor a request to cater a party or reception in Los Angeles or Palm Springs? Should I say, "We just don't go that far!"? I figured that Riverside was a half hour away and Palm Springs, about an hour. Therefore, it only takes a half hour longer to get to Palm Springs. By looking at it that way, I decided distance was not a factor. Soon we began to go anywhere. I even catered my niece's wedding in Florida. We made lasagna and meatballs in California, froze it, packed it in boxes, and transported it, along with other essential supplies—like paper plates, cutlery, napkins, and tablecloths, on the plane. In those days, the airlines allowed two boxes per person, and since four of us were going to the wedding, we were able to haul everything at no additional cost. In Florida, my wife and I finished preparations at the hall, and served 250 to 300 guests our lasagna and meatballs, which thawed out as we were flying there. Everyone thought we did a beautiful job.

I noticed early in my catering days that most of my competitors did not have facilities or kitchens of their own. They worked out of their homes, garages, or storage facilities, and could only take jobs that had kitchens of their own. I discovered by watching them do it their way, that it is more efficient to cook, wash, and clean up in one kitchen for multiple parties than in several different kitchens for individual parties. It takes more labor, and more personnel, and is not as effective as the way I have been doing it.

Many people ask me for a good recipe for chicken. There must be over a 1,000 ways to prepare chicken, but I always say, "Just add salt, pepper, and garlic, and bake it in the oven and it will be the best chicken you have ever eaten." Sometimes, the simplest way is the best—another valuable lesson I have learned.

And also that every man should eat and drink, and enjoy the good of all his labour, it is a gift of God.

—Ecc. 3:13

32

I Love A Vacation

I HAVE ALWAYS LOVED TO TRAVEL, but my favorite vacations of late have been ones with the entire family—kids and grandkids included. We took our first trip together to Hawaii in 2002. Jack, the owner of Los Caballeros, allowed us to use his five-bedroom, waterfront pool home on the big island of Hawaii. The next year, my wife and I took ten of our grandchildren on a cruise to the Mexican Riviera—without their parents. When we travel with the parents, we feel somewhat denied, so this gave us the opportunity to spend time with our grandkids alone. By far, this was the best vacation my wife and I have ever taken. I cannot tell you how much fun it was being with Michael, Christy, Mike, Nick, Vince, Brian, AJ, Uriel, Alison, and Alexandra, both aboard ship and on shore.

The Mastroianni grandkids on a cruise with Jay and Eleanor

The not-too-distant Mexico became one of our favorite vacation destinations beginning in 1962. My wife and I traveled to Mexico City and visited Guadalajara, but our favorite spot was in Puerto Vallarta. Over the years, we have returned there many times. I took my sons fishing in Puerto Vallarta every chance I got, and Michael, in particular, developed a love for the sport. Back home in Newport Beach, we fished open from charter boats on trips used to "wine and dine" our business clients.

Since Mercury Savings President Leonard Shane and I had quickly become friends, I was honored when, in 1986, he invited me, along with 29 others, to his grandson's bar mitzvah in Israel! The bar mitzvah was held at the Wailing Wall, and the dinner at the Jerusalem Hilton. I was delighted to find that our Jerusalem hotel rivaled 5-star hotels anywhere in the world.

A few years earlier, in 1976, I took my father to visit his hometown of Gizzeria, Italy. I had always wanted to see it for myself. The town was located on a hill, and could be seen from the beach below. It was only a mile away, but we had to drive 12 miles up a winding road to get there. My father had left Gizzeria 57 years before. As he looked over the town and his house, which was over 400 years old, he was disheartened by the fact that the little village was still as drab and forlorn as he remembered it.

I was surprised at how many relatives my father had there. My dad was a good man, and for years, had been sending money back to poor relatives in his old village. They loved and respected him for providing for them. We met my paternal uncle's son and the children and grandchildren of a sister, who had died a few months earlier. My father had not spoken to her since he left Italy because she had a child out of wedlock years earlier and his upbringing would not condone it. His nephew insisted we go see her children anyway, and I am glad we did. They were the kindest people and treated us well. Visiting my father's hometown was another memorable experience in my life— made even more special because I shared it with my father.

> *A man that has friends must show himself friendly.*
>
> —Pro. 18:22

33

Vacationing In New York On 9/11

I have been friends with Leo and Virginia Zlaket for a long time. They own Zlaket's Market on Main Street in Garden Grove, where his family has been in business for 76 years. Our family businesses created a bond between us, and we had always talked about going on vacation together. To celebrate my birthday in September of 2001, we decided to take a trip to New York City. Leo and his wife vacation in New York City all the time, so my wife and I was delighted to go with someone who could show us around.

We left on a Thursday and checked into the Hilton Hotel on Sixth Avenue late in the afternoon. The next day, we toured the city, including Wall Street and South Street Seaport where we took pictures of the Brooklyn Bridge and the New York skyline, with the twin towers of the World Trade Center in the distance. Our plans for Sunday included a visit to Long Island for a family party, arranged by my Cousin Dominic's son that I had planned to host. I had lived with his father and his grandmother for four years when I was 17. We took the Long Island Railroad to Westbury, and Dominic did not know we were coming. He thought he was merely having dinner with his immediate family. When he entered the restaurant and saw me, he was overcome with emotion. It was quite a family reunion.

On Monday, we arose early to see the taping of the Regis & Kelly Show, which is broadcast near Lincoln Square. That evening, September 10, we had dinner reservations at Peter Lugar's Steak House, a 45-minute rainy cab ride over the Brooklyn Bridge. The restaurant was over 100 years old, and we enjoyed great food and a pleasant evening there. We were having a wonderful time!

The next morning, September 11, 2001, I awoke to my wife shaking me and screaming, "Look what's happening outside!" We were only a few blocks from the World Trade Center, on the fifteenth floor of the Hilton, not in any immediate danger, but shaken by the tragedy that we were watching unfold in front of us. Our plans had been to leave New York City that day, but as everyone may recall, no one could get out of New York for days. We sat glued to the television most of the time, wondering if we would ever get home. It was hard to believe that we were in New York City witnessing one of the most tragic events of the 21st Century from our hotel room window. We had to wait four days before we could get a flight back to California from Newark, New Jersey. We still have our unused tickets to the Broadway musical, "42nd Street," as a reminder of the trip.

Besides the trauma of what had happened at the World Trade Center, I was feeling very tired and had trouble keeping up with my wife, Leo and Virginia while we were in New York. It is not surprising, because two weeks later, I ended up in the hospital with heart problems.

New York City—
the calm before the storm

The Zlakets and Mastroiannis in New York

> *Yet he sets the poor on high from affliction, and makes him families like a flock.*
>
> —Psalm 107:41

34

From 10 to 80 in 50 Years

Our move to California took place nearly 50 years ago, and I had a real concern that it would be a lonely existence for us, even though my sister Rose was here with her family. That did not prove to be right. Soon after we moved here, my sisters-in-law Betty and Dorothy, along with their husbands and children, followed us to the Golden State. A few nieces and nephews from Pennsylvania came and stayed for a while, but most returned home, except for Roz Silva, my wife's niece (Frank Barco's daughter). She came to California in 1978 and stayed to raise a family.

There were ten or twelve of us in the early days. For the first few years, we would have potlucks on special occasions and holidays. One of us would cook the turkey, and someone would bring spaghetti. I know that is not a good combination, but Italian tradition says you always have to have spaghetti. My sister-in-law Dorothy loved to sing and play the accordion but was not fond of cooking. Most of the parties were at our house or Betty's.

One year, I told Dorothy that I was inviting myself to her house for Christmas and I would come in a tuxedo to celebrate the rare occasion. I did, and everyone had a good laugh. At our Thanksgiving potluck one year, it was Dorothy's turn to cook the turkey. When dinner time approached, Dorothy and her husband had not shown up or even called to explain their absence. We had to eat Thanksgiving dinner without the turkey! When we finally asked what the problem was, she told us she and her husband had a terrible fight and did not have a chance to cook the turkey, much less bring it over. Whenever we get together as a family, we love to tell the story of how Dorothy failed to show up with our holiday turkey.

Our extended family has grown from ten family members to nearly 80. We do not have those potlucks anymore, but have to rent a hall if we want to have a get-together. It has been a real joy to watch all the nieces, nephews and cousins grow up. Today, there are more of my wife's family members here in California than in Pennsylvania. Except for my brother-in-law Ted Flati, Betty's husband, who died in 1990, we still have all our original members. I doubt anyone ever regrets making the cross-country move because we have all done well. Dorothy and her husband, Jesse, are the creator/owners of the Blue Book, a guide for insurance claims adjustors, which now employs all of their four children, Marilyn, Danny, Mark, and Michela. Ted Flati, before his death, enjoyed a successful career in business, while Betty was raising their five children, Joanne, Ted, Terri, Matt, and Richard, and helping us at Jay's. California has been good to us.

Jesse, Dorothy, Eleanor, Jay, Betty and Ted

"A good man leaves an inheritance to his children's children."

—Pro. 13:22

35

Who In The Family Will Succeed?

Many years ago, I attended a seminar in San Francisco on family businesses, and one of the things I learned was that only 10 percent of family enterprises succeed to the third generation. That statistic has never left my mind. I have often wondered if our business would be in that lucky 10 percent, but I think I have the answer.

In the past year, I have witnessed my daughter Linda as she competently runs the business, yet all the while, giving her son, Michael Ring, more of an opportunity to learn. She has increased his day-to-day responsibilities, and Michael is succeeding in many areas. It is wonderful to watch what goes on between mother and son. They work together well as he shows complete respect for his mother. I have never once witnessed a disagreement between them. Michael has worked full-time at *Jay's* for ten years and is knowledgeable in all facets of the business. He started as a server, moved on to scheduling and event management and then, into sales, which he quickly mastered. Michael continues to affect Jay's with his bright ideas and strong work ethic. He recently held a server seminar at our house. I was so impressed that when the servers left, I cried when I realized the improvement in the level of our service over the last 40 years. What Michael showed me was incredible. I believe his goal, which I saw on his face, is to achieve the epitome of excellence in service for *Jay's*

Catering. Just as his mother became my "heir apparent" when her two brothers found their future in catering golf tournaments, I believe Michael will follow his mother into management, although Linda has never said so. He recently became a Board of Director member of our company.

A long time ago, I decided that no matter who succeeded me, the deal would be this: "He who works, gets paid. He, who does not work, gets profit-sharing." Thus today, my sons and their children, as well as Linda's children, are shareholders in the company. As shareholders, I want them to stay involved in *Jay's Catering*, and more importantly, active in the community. I would like to see them join service organizations, such as Kiwanis, or the local Chamber of Commerce. This will not only benefit them personally, as they meet new friends and gain contacts, but also help foster future business possibilities for our company. Even if they do not work at Jay's, they can act as spokespersons and representatives of the company they own and continue to support the family members who do operate the company on a daily basis. I pray they will be generous with what they have been given and give back to society. Making contributions to needy organizations is essential in any man's life, but particularly when you are in business.

I know that God gave each one of them unique talents and gifts, and has led them down different paths to college and careers. It is a blessing to see each of them on their own, working toward these goals and dreams. Still, it is my desire that my grandchildren remain close, no matter where their careers and families may take them. Like my father before me, I hope and pray they will see the importance of family, both immediate and extended.

Linda's son Michael

Linda's kids—(rear) Michael, AJ, Brian, Uriel Jr., (front) Jacob, Gina, Christy

"...a man cannot tell what shall be; and what shall be after him, who can tell him?"

— Ecc. 10:14

36

Family Matters

As I have already mentioned, my father's dream was for us to work together in a family business, and that has happened to me. My three children have never worked anywhere else—only for the family business or themselves. We have had our trials and tribulations, but "family first" continues to be our motto.

In addition, my father's message was intended for my brother and sisters as well. As I mentioned, my brother Emilio Mastroianni or Amo, was in the service station business for 45 years in Rochester, Pa. By the time he retired, he had received many honors from Esso Gasoline, for salesmanship and service. He did very well for himself. My sister, Grace Raso, has five daughters and every one is a college graduate.

My sister's husband Joe opened a real estate office in Cape Coral, Florida, 45 years ago, and four of the five girls are in the business. When he died, he left the business to his eldest daughter, who turned it over to her son, my sister's grandson.

My sister Rose Roppa, who passed away about 10 years ago, had a dry cleaning business in Santa Ana for years. My father made her quit school in tenth grade, so she could run our Italian grocery store in 1941. This was his first attempt at a family business, but unfortunately, it did not succeed. The lesson was not lost on her because in addition to her dry cleaning business, she owned a restaurant in Tustin before she died. Her daughter Tina owns a maple furniture manufacturing plant in Northern California, Carol Anne works for an attorney in Los Angeles, and her son Carmen formerly owned a truck catering business.

The entrepreneurial spirit has definitely thrived in our family, much to the delight of my father, Giovanni, who lived until he was 95 and did witness many of these family business ventures before his death in 1986.

The siblings—Amo, Grace, Jay, Rose (seated)

> *In everything, give thanks,*
> *for this is the will of God.*
>
> — 1 Thes. 5:18

37

Near Death

In the fall of 2004, I was treated at Orange Coast Hospital in Fountain Valley for a persistent stomach infection. During my stay, I fell off the bed one night while heavily medicated. I had no idea how long I lay on the floor or that I had been injured, but an MRI (Magnetic Resonance Imaging) revealed that my No. 2, 3 and 4 discs, located in the neck area, were pressing on my spine. From there, I was hospitalized for the original infection at Hoag Hospital and then the Tustin Rehabilitation Center for gout. My neck continued to be a problem, and upon further review, my doctor theorized I could become paralyzed if I moved it the wrong way. He strongly recommended surgery, although the heart specialist did not believe I was strong enough to handle it.

When I was feeling better, I sought two or three more opinions and eventually took the recommendation of a UCLA doctor, who believed that it was indeed a dangerous surgery, but that the risk of paralysis was worse. He explained that I would spend two, maybe three days, in the hospital recuperating after surgery. I prepared for a short hospitalization in May 2005. Although the surgery went well, I did experience cardiac arrest two days later. My wife and son Michael were in the room alone with me at the time and became very frightened when they realized what was happening. They called for the nurse, who issued a Code Blue. The hospital staff arrived immediately to work on saving my life. Apparently, my throat swelled due to the surgery, closing off my air passages, making it impossible for me to breathe, and resulting in cardiac arrest. The doctors revived me, but it was necessary to sedate me heavily for the next several weeks.

My family pulled together and did everything to make sure I received the best care possible. Eleanor stayed by my bedside constantly—even renting rooms at a nearby hotel so she would not have to make the 90-mile roundtrip drive along some of southern California's busiest freeways. Linda made a schedule to ensure a family member was always in my room. My sons, daughters-in-law, and grandkids all came to UCLA to help. After three weeks, I was transferred to a re-habilitation center. I do not remember anything until I woke up in an ambulance on the way to the Tustin Rehabilitation Center. I had not seen my wife from the day I went into cardiac arrest until I arrived at the center. When I finally saw her, I started to cry because she looked so pale and drawn even though I was the sick one. I could not believe what a toll my illness had taken on her.

My sister-in-law Betty and our friend, Valerie King, my brother-in-law and sister-in-law Jesse and Dorothy, all Bible-believing Christians, came and prayed for me on several occasions. They just wanted me to get well. One day Valerie said, "When this is all over, Jay, we have to have Prayer Appreciation Day," and I thought that made good sense. During my illness, Eleanor told me I received nearly 150 get-well cards, and the receptionist jokingly complained that the phone at Jay's never stopped ringing with inquiries about my health.

It took me three months to recuperate from my illness. When I was well enough, I took Valerie up on her suggestion to thank everyone for their prayers, cards and support by having a Prayer Appreciation lunch. In November 2005, 200 family members and friends gathered at *Los Caballeros* for that party. That celebration took place over a year ago, and I continue to recover. I am able to do things today that I could have only imagined a year ago.

We live our years as
a tale that is told.

— Psalm 90: 9

38

A Story Unfolds

My wife and I have been married for 53 years now. I once took into account the different qualities she and I possess to see what made us successful in business. Eleanor is honest, friendly, intelligent, educated, family-oriented, loyal, and supportive. She has common sense, patience, and kindness. I, on the other hand, have perseverance, diligence, an entrepreneurial spirit, vision, faith, integrity, honesty, enthusiasm, and common sense. Although my wife and I originally had entirely different goals in life, when we put our heads together, we came up with a formula for success. She was a wonderful cook and I was a great salesman.

We recently celebrated the high school and college graduations of three of our grandsons, granddaughter, two great nephews, and several wives and girlfriends with a big family party for relatives, including many from Pennsylvania and Florida in June 2006. Guests of honor also included the parents of the girl from Ohio my grandson was marrying shortly after the party.

In honor of the occasion, I compiled a short history of our family—including names of grandparents and great grandparents on both sides—because I wanted my grandkids to know the history behind their family name. Later on, that short history provided the inspiration to fill in the details of my nearly eight decades on this earth. As I have had the opportunity to re-live my past, I have discovered that I have everything I always wanted:

— the love of a good woman, who knows how to cook and nurse me back to health when I am ill,

— a profession that allowed me to exercise my creativity,

— a daughter so determined and competent that she runs this multi-million dollar company with the greatest of ease, in addition to raising five of the most intelligent, loving grandchildren one man could ask for,

— two sons, who are not only professional salesmen and successful marketers, but also faithful husbands and incredibly devoted fathers,

— a host of loyal employees,

— plus kind relatives and generous friends,

— and satisfied customers who keep coming back.

Eleanor and Jay

Epilogue

Some people know exactly what they want to be in life and go after it; others fall into a job they like and spend the rest of their days doing it; yet, still more individuals follow their fathers or family into the same line of work. I had no clue what I wanted to be. I did not become a gardener like my father (although my sister Rose's husband Tom became Superintendent of Landscaping at Disneyland); did not enjoy the gas station business like my brother, Amo, and never happened upon a job I enjoyed until my wife and I started preparing and serving food for other people. I do believe that every occupation I had gave me the skills to do what I do—cater. For instance, my job as a shoe repairmen taught me patience and persistence at getting something just right; being a milkman showed me how to be friendly to people from all walks of life; as a service station attendant, I learned to move quickly and get the job done; being a delivery man again taught me diligence and perseverance. Owning a truck catering business forced me to deal with all sorts of people, from drivers to suppliers to customers.

In looking back, I now see that I was a jack-of-all-trades, with an entrepreneurial spirit, which I exercised every chance I got. However, it was not until I found the right occupation, and the shoe fit (to borrow a phrase from my past profession) that I finally became a master of one! For me, it was persistence, coupled with a certain amount of failure, that in the end, made me successful.

I also find it amusing that until I was 45 years old, I had two good arms, a strong back and a sharp mind, but I could not get ahead. Then, after almost going bankrupt, breaking my arm and my wrist so severely that I could never sign my name again, and suffering for a year with a chronic illness, I began to reap the benefits of my lifelong struggle to find success.